GHOST RIDERS
IN THE SKY

THE LIFE OF STAN JONES, THE SINGING RANGER

Michael K. Ward

RIO NUEVO PUBLISHERS
TUCSON, AZ

Rio Nuevo Publishers®
P. O. Box 5250
Tucson, AZ 85703-0250
(520) 623-9558, www.rionuevo.com

Library of Congress Cataloging-in-Publication Data

Ward, Michael K., 1952- author.
  Ghost riders in the sky : the life of Stan Jones, the singing ranger / Michael K. Ward.
    pages cm
  Includes bibliographical references and index.
  ISBN 978-1-933855-99-8 (pbk.) — ISBN 1-933855-99-1
  1. Jones, Stan, 1914-1963. 2. Composers—United States—Biography. 3. Singers—United States—Biography.
  4. Country musicians—United States—Biography. I. Title.
  ML410.J737W37 2014
  782.421642092—dc23
  [B]   2014014921

Book design: Preston Thomas, Cadence Design Studio
Cover design: David Jenney Design

Printed in the United States of America.

10 9 8 7 6 5 4 3 2 1

CONTENTS

FOREWORD BY RANGER DOUG   *v*
PROLOGUE   *vii*

CHAPTER 1   Douglas, Arizona   *1*
CHAPTER 2   Young Riders   *11*
CHAPTER 3   In the Navy   *17*
CHAPTER 4   Cowboy, Change Your Ways   *25*
CHAPTER 5   Mount Rainier   *33*
CHAPTER 6   A Hot, Miserable, Godforsaken Hole   *41*
CHAPTER 7   No Water in That Cactus   *55*
CHAPTER 8   Nature Boy   *63*
CHAPTER 9   All the Stars of Death Valley   *71*
CHAPTER 10   We Hope He Makes a Million Dollars   *83*
CHAPTER 11   Don't Write Anything about Cactus!   *93*
CHAPTER 12   Silver Screen Songwriter   *105*
CHAPTER 13   I'm No Actor   *115*
CHAPTER 14   Creakin' Leather   *125*
CHAPTER 15   Song of the Trail   *135*
CHAPTER 16   Roll Along   *143*
CHAPTER 17   You Never Really Ever Died   *153*
CHAPTER 18   Ghost Riders in the Sky   *163*

EPILOGUE   *173*
GHOST RIDERS IN THE SKY LYRICS   *175*
ACKNOWLEDGMENTS   *177*
NOTES   *181*
SUGGESTED READING   *189*
INDEX   *194*

FOREWORD

BACK WHEN GENE AUTRY'S SUDDEN AND UNEXPECTED SUCCESS MADE the musical western hugely popular, studios and labels rushed to find not only new singing cowboys but also new songs for them to sing. Into this void rushed dozens of gifted young men and women, and talents like Andy Parker, Johnny Bond, Billy Hill, Smiley Burnette, and Ray Whitley wrote timeless classics. In fact, most of the singing cowboys wrote many of their songs, most notably Gene Autry, as well as Eddie Dean, Jimmy Wakely, Rex Allen, Foy Willing, and Tex Ritter. They were creating an entirely new genre of music focusing not on love relationships, not on the work of the cowboy, but on the beauty and majesty of the West itself.

Head and shoulders above these greatly talented people stand three giants in the field of western songwriting: Bob Nolan, Tim Spencer, and Stan Jones. Nolan's and Spencer's contributions have been detailed in at least two fine histories of the Sons of the Pioneers, and Nolan's legacy is maintained in a superb website, www.bobnolan-sop.net. But until now little was known about the genial park ranger who wrote many of the most poetic, memorable, and beautiful portraits of the west: Stan Jones.

Jones's peripatetic and all too short life has at last been documented in this superbly researched and written biography. Mike Ward has done monumental homework tracking down the many loose ends, chronological gaps, and missing months and years in Jones's vagabond life. But more importantly he writes, and writes well, of music, poetry, and the creative process with understanding and insight.

This is a volume that needed to be written, a life that needed to be explored. I envy your journey through Stan Jones's remarkable life and world and art, and tip my hat to the work, the skill, and the love Mike Ward has devoted to bringing Stan Jones's remarkable legacy to lovers of western music around the world.

—RANGER DOUG of Riders in the Sky,
Honorary National Park Service Ranger

PROLOGUE

ON A QUIET SUNDAY MORNING, STAN JONES SAT IN A WOODEN CHAIR underneath the front porch overhang of the Emigrant ranger station. He casually strummed his four-stringed Martin guitar slung over his shoulder by a frayed cord of manila rope. Beneath the vast blanket of sky, a dark alluvial jumble of volcanic boulders and scraggly creosotes sloped steeply down to the far northeastern reaches of Death Valley. Stan and his wife Olive had called the stone ranger station home since the previous fall of 1946. Emigrant served as Stan's base of operations as a park service ranger, from which he patrolled the vast and remote Death Valley National Monument in his government Ford pickup.

Stan trained his eyes toward the distant patch of ancient lakebed that lay splashed across the valley floor, while gently running his fingers across the strings of his guitar, absorbing the deep contentment of the moment. He was in his early thirties, settled with the woman he loved, holding a dream job as a ranger in the immense desert wilderness that extended out before him. It had been a ragged, oftentimes rough journey for Ranger Jones before reaching the place of peace that he gratefully savored that morning.

Singing and songwriting had become a passion of Stan's thanks to Olive's encouragement and her gift of the Martin tenor guitar that he held in his hands. When the spirit moved him, he composed songs that were often inspired by his youthful memories of roaming the border frontier of southeastern Arizona. On this particular morning, Stan began to muse about a vision that had haunted his imagination since he was a boy in the mid-1920s. He fiddled with a couple of chord progressions, hit on a melody that seemed to match, and then began to put a few lines together in his head. In about ten minutes he had the makings of what he thought was a pretty good song. "Ollie!" he called to his wife inside, "you'd better write this down!"

That song was destined to become one of the most enduring and memorable American ballads of all time, "Ghost Riders in the Sky."

CHAPTER 1

DOUGLAS, ARIZONA

*One June evening in 1914 while Pancho Villa was busy shooting up
a Mexican border town, a newborn citizen lustily joined in the din
from a little Arizona ranch house about 200 yards away. Stan Jones
had just arrived.*
   —Arizona Highways, 1957

WHOA, HOLD YOUR HORSES THERE, PARDNER! THAT'S STRETCHING
things a little bit far . . .

It is a fact that Stan Jones was born in the Cochise County border town
of Douglas, Arizona, in June of 1914. The future songwriter was more likely
swaddled in diapers and hollering for a bottle by November of 1915 when
Villa and his army commenced their attack against Mexican federal troops
across the border in Agua Prieta. The unassuming cottage on Eighth Street
where Stan had first opened his eyes bore little resemblance to a ranch house
and stood less than a mile from the international border a few blocks from
downtown Douglas.

Stan's family roots lay in the Deep South. His father, Jonathon Edmond
Jones, was born of Welsh descent in Florida in 1866. John met and married
sixteen-year-old Berta Margaret Davis in Rockport, Texas, in 1891. Described
by a grandson as being "very Southern," Stan's mother, who preferred to be
called Berta, was born in Georgia in 1874 and swore she was a blood relative

G. Ave., Looking South from 10th St., Douglas, Ariz.

Douglas street scene, circa 1916. *Courtesy of Cochise County Historical Society*

of a couple of the main players in the "War between the States." Naturally, with the surname of Davis, she proudly proclaimed that the President of the Confederacy was her granduncle. Then, with contrary disgust, Berta also disclosed her bloodlines to George McClellan, who she cast as "a bad general and a damn Yankee."

Berta bore four children in Texas between 1893 and 1902: Clara, Nell, Malcomb, and Jack. By 1906, the family resided in El Paso, Texas, while John Jones was employed at a Mexican gold and silver mine in Ocampo, in the Mexican state of Coahuila. Berta's efforts to instill a love of music and an affinity for church in her children are reflected in a letter that nine-year-old Nell Jones sent to her father in Mexico. She shared that "We are going to start Sunday school next Sunday. Do they have Sunday school in Ocampo?" and that "Clara and I went to a little entertainment yesterday [where] we saw a little boy eight years old play the piano beautifully." As an adult Nell recalled her father as a "kind of troubadour," sporting "a wonderful baritone voice," and that her brothers and sisters were "enchanted by the way Father could spin a yarn and sing."

In 1907, Jones accepted a job as a mercantile clerk at Cananea Consolidated Copper Company in Mexico, not far from Douglas, Arizona, where Berta's younger brother Grover Davis worked as an engineer for the Phelps Dodge Copper Queen Smelter. Berta and John had a fifth child, Jeanne,

(LEFT) John Edmond Jones, age 24. (RIGHT) Berta Davis Jones, age 16, probably taken in 1891 shortly after their marriage. *Courtesy of Bill Dubs*

born in Cananea in 1908. Eventually Nell, Malcomb, and Jack moved on to Douglas, either to work or attend school. By 1912, only Jeanne and Clara remained with their parents in Mexico.

The town of Douglas, snug against the Mexican border, was incorporated in 1901. Abundant ground water and a reasonable proximity to nearby Phelps Dodge copper mines, particularly the Copper Queen in Bisbee, made Douglas a logical location for large-scale smelter operations. Cattle ranching and farming were the predominant economic forces in the relatively lawless region before the arrival of the railroads and the Phelps Dodge Corporation. The first decade of the twentieth century found Douglas teetering between a rough frontier heritage and its burgeoning respectability as a thriving business community.

By 1913, political unrest and sporadic violence in Cananea as a result of the ongoing Mexican Revolution drove John Jones and his remaining brood across the border to Douglas, where they decamped to Grover Davis's home at 914 Eighth Street. Berta Jones dutifully registered to vote in the city that then contained a population of approximately 7,000 citizens, and recorded that she possessed dark hair and grey eyes, stood 5 feet tall, and weighed 120

Four of Stan's older siblings with Berta, 1902. From left to right: Clara, Nell, Malcomb, Berta, and Jack. *Courtesy of Keeter Stuart*

pounds. She found herself unexpectedly pregnant that fall, and Stanley Davis Jones, diplomatically referred to as an "afterthought" by one of his nephews, was born on June 5 the following year at the house on Eighth Street. His birth certificate lists his father's age as forty-seven and his occupation as store manager. Berta is recorded as a thirty-nine-year-old housewife.

Stan was baptized at St. Stephen's Episcopal Church, July 12, 1914, as witnessed by his godparents, Grover Davis, and two family friends associated with the Copper Queen smelter. Stan never knew his father. John Jones drifted away from Douglas, choosing to turn his back on Berta, his newborn son, and the cramped confines of Grover's home. In 1919, Berta received an uncontested divorce from her husband and then discreetly listed herself as the widow of J. E. Jones in the Douglas city directory in an effort to avoid the social stain of being a divorcée. Stan's father eventually settled in Prescott, Arizona, where he worked as a grocer, before dying of cancer in 1927.

Clara Jones took a job as a bookkeeper at the Phelps Dodge Mercantile and helped her mother support Jeanne and Stan in their father's absence. The family moved into a house of their own at 946 Fourteenth Street, the dwelling that Stan would affectionately remember in his later years as his childhood home. By April of 1921, the postwar demand for copper had

Stan as a young boy in Douglas (date unknown). *Courtesy of Bill Dubs and Pamela Moritz*

nosedived and smelter operations in Douglas were temporarily shut down. Clara had managed to retain her job at Phelps Dodge and agreed to continue fostering her younger sister Jeanne in Douglas when their mother moved to El Paso, shifting the burden of support for Berta and seven-year-old Stan to his brothers, Malcomb and Jack. The following year, 1922, Clara married Clarence Hinton, the son of Douglas mayor A. E. Hinton. Berta's continued embarrassment at being divorced from her husband was reflected in the Douglas newspaper's announcement of the wedding, in which Clara was listed as being the daughter of "Mr. and Mrs. J. E. Jones of El Paso."

The liaison via marriage with the Hinton family brought a heightened respectability to the splintered Jones clan. Mayor Hinton, a stalwart leader of Douglas's Democratic Party, had ventured to the Arizona Territory in 1883 from Kansas, settled in Phoenix by 1886, and in the 1890s served a term in the Arizona Territorial Legislature. He moved down to Douglas and by 1908 began a long career at the Phelps Dodge Copper Queen smelter, holding a

variety of posts until his retirement in 1931. A committed civic activist, he
served as the mayor of Douglas beginning in 1920, before his election to the
state legislature in 1928. His son Clarence served overseas in the military
during World War I, then returned to a job as chief clerk in the supply
department at the smelter. After his marriage to Clara, Clarence generously
agreed to absorb her fitful mother and young brother into his household.
When Berta and Stan returned to Douglas in 1923, the sizable Hinton residence on Thirteenth Street became their new address.

Standing on the threshold of adolescence at the age of nine, Stan now
enjoyed the semblance of a steady domestic setting from which to explore
his ever-widening world. Despite inheriting aspects of his mother's chronic
nervous condition, marked by sporadic episodes of sleepwalking and the
tendency to suffer from nightmares, Stan soldiered through his classes as
a middling student at the A Avenue Elementary School. Lacking a socially
conventional family unit, Stan was able to mosey about town a bit more
freely than many of his classmates. He had a natural bent toward showmanship
and in all likelihood tried harder than most kids to be accepted due to his
chagrin at being a fatherless boy. The cocky, slightly rebellious aura about
him fomented whispers in the parlors of proper Douglas society that Stan
was "the kind of little boy mothers didn't want their sons to play with."

At an early age, Stan displayed his father's talent for storytelling. A neighbor, Gladys Acosta, recalls that the sandy-haired, "very good looking" boy
would line the local kids up at dusk along the high curbs designed to accommodate the torrential summer cloudbursts. While they dangled their
feet above the concrete gutter, Stan would spin a ghost story he invented
and proceed to scare the daylights out of his wide-eyed little audience. She
remembered, "We had to listen, and then our mothers would call us and we
would all be afraid to go home." Ms. Acosta also witnessed Stan heroically
saving a neighborhood boy's life:

> There was a boy who lived across the street from us, Tommy Wright. He
> and another boy were taking some cleaning fluid out and they lit a match.
> Some of the fluid had spilled on Tommy's pant leg. He caught on fire and
> started running. Stan tackled him. If it hadn't been for Stan, he would have
> burned to death.

Thanks to his mother, Stan's education blossomed beyond the walls of
the classroom and his local neighborhood haunts. Berta Jones doggedly

impressed upon her youngest child a devotion to church, and at the St. Stephen's Episcopal Church where he had been baptized, Stan came under the sway of the charismatic Reverend Ernest W. Simonson. A Canadian by birth, the Reverend Simonson arrived in Douglas in 1906 to take over a church that consisted of a paltry fourteen members. By the time of Stan's birth in 1914, Simonson, renowned for his boundless energy, had built a loyal following of approximately 350 civically active parishioners who collectively viewed their spiritual leader as the "ideal priest." Stan attended services regularly, became an acolyte, and years later boasted, "I carried the cross there for ten years."

In addition to his church activities, Stan was coming of age at just the right time to experience a blossoming influence on American boyhood: the Boy Scouts of America. Scoutmaster Charles A. Nichols moved to Douglas from upstate New York in the early 1900s and established a laundry service. He was a vestry member of St. Stephen's parish and a fervent promoter of the relatively new national organization. As he recruited eager youngsters from the church for his scout troop, Stan jumped on board to take the scout oath and, at the age of ten, immersed himself in the practical skills of wilderness navigation, wielding an axe, and surviving snakebites.

Nichols was the driving force behind establishing Camp Victorio, a summer retreat for scouts high in a meadow called Rustler's Park in the Chiricahua Mountains, north of Douglas. Nichols explained the choice of Victorio for the name of the camp in his *Introduction To Pageants And Rituals For Cochise Council*. He wrote, "The Council finally selected the name 'Victorio,' not particularly because he was the most blood-thirsty of the Apache chiefs but because his hunting ground was located in these mountains." A verse from a poem written by Nichols extolling the scouts' mountain hideaway reads: "Legends of Apache days / Romance in the air / Rustler's Park and haunted camp / Mystery everywhere."

Nichols was consumed by a melodramatic enchantment with the Apache legacy of the region. One activity at Camp Victorio included the scouts acting in elaborate skits written by Nichols. He sought "not only to encourage the study of Indian lore but also to interpret the Boy Scout Laws, Indian fashion." Prominent landmarks of the region served as the settings for his dramas. All scouts were keyed in to the locations of the "red caves of the rising sun" at Cave Creek, the "valley of the white waters" at the southern end of the Sulphur Springs Valley, and the Cochise Stronghold, "the last fortification and burial place of Old Cochise," across the Willcox Playa in the Dragoon Mountains.

An operatic blend of frontier myth and authentic history, Nichols's primary opus was *Dear Old Cochise: A Pageant in Three Acts*. The cast included Apache chiefs Mangas Coloradas, Geronimo, and Cochise, starring alongside a host of U.S. cavalrymen, in a theatric rendering of the clashes between the historic frontier protagonists. His plays typically glossed over the rampant brutality displayed by all sides in a conflict that eventually led to the banishment of the Apaches from their traditional homelands. Nichols painted the Apache warriors in "noble savage" brushstrokes that complemented the marked influence that American Indian culture played in guiding the creation of the Boy Scouts of America.

Between honing his scouting talents in the rugged wilds of the Chiricahuas and acting out his scoutmaster's heroic Apache War dramas, young Stan was beginning to accumulate a rich brew of practical knowledge and experience that would ultimately serve him well as both a ranger and a songwriter. Genial raconteur Mayor A. E. Hinton frequently visited Clarence and Clara's home on Thirteenth Street, calmly enthralling the assembled household with largely unadorned stories of his adventures on the Arizona frontier as a green seventeen-year-old from Kansas. In the 1880s he had labored as a swamper (driver's assistant) on a freight wagon pulled by a combined team of eighteen mules and horses, hauling supplies from Willcox to Globe and back. Stan loved to hear of Hinton's ridiculously oversized sombrero that he had bought for his trip west and how a band of Apache boys had used it for target practice one evening along the Gila River. Hinton recalled being grateful that the huge hat wasn't on his head as the arrows flew. These recollections by the mayor provided young Stan with an unidealized, true-to-life counterpoint to the mawkish nostalgia of the Native American scenarios promoted by Charlie Nichols.

Early editions of the *Boy Scout Handbook* opened another doorway of discovery for Stan. Not only could a determined lad learn how to start a fire without a match or negotiate the confusing hurdles of puberty but, with a few simple tools and inexpensive materials, a scout could follow the instructions supplied in the *Handbook* to build a crystal radio receiver and a sending unit. Modern teenagers don't have a lock on obsessive fascination with new technologies. In the mid-1920s, radio was an exciting cutting-edge invention, and for Stan and a couple of his best friends drawn from the orderly grids of his Douglas neighborhood, radio became a lifelong hobby. Stan could often be found huddled over soldering irons with pals Wayne Hester and John Kendricks, constructing homemade transmitter units in a corner of Kendricks's father's garage.

When they weren't fiddling with radio equipment, the three boys earned a little money doing an assortment of jobs. Hester helped on a milk truck run, and Kendricks maintained a paper route along the border between Douglas and Agua Prieta. Stan hawked newspapers on a downtown corner, worked part-time at Ferguson's Drug Store on G Street, and cared for a few lawns owned by St. Stephen's parishioners. Stan's mother had a job as a bookkeeper for a plumbing company by 1926, but money was perpetually tight. Later in his life, Stan groused about being the only child in his family who hadn't received any formal music training. However, what he gained in lieu of piano lessons was the exhilarating freedom to roam the rugged Chihuahuan desert borderlands. This landscape, freshly haunted by the cowboy and Indian legends of a turbulent, dangerous frontier, served as inspirational proving grounds for the future author of western songs and ballads.

CHAPTER 2

YOUNG RIDERS

WITHIN STAN'S CIRCLE OF CITY FRIENDS, OWNING A HORSE WAS OUT of the question for both economic and practical reasons. The perfect alternative for playing cowpoke was wandering untethered on the outskirts of town. Burros, abandoned for the warmer months of the year by Mexican woodcutters, became the steeds of choice for aspiring Douglas cowpunchers. Unfettered by school responsibilities during their summer break, Stan and his sidekicks urged their commandeered burros out to the cattle ranches scattered among the low rises of the Perilla Mountains east of town.

Douglas and the surrounding territory had been rough country only two or three decades previously. Thomas Rynning, captain of the Arizona Rangers who set up shop in Douglas in 1902, had this to say about the local Cochise County denizens:

> I've been in many a tough town in my day, but from Deadwood to Tombstone I've never met with a harder formation than Douglas was. . . . Cattle thieves, murderers, all the worst hombres of the United States and Mexico made their headquarters there. The dance-halls were the worst I've seen on any frontier.

Geronimo and his renegade band of Chiricahua Apaches had finally been harassed by the U.S. Army into surrendering and were deported from the region by 1886. Practically every Arizonan who had weathered the terrors of that era had a story to tell—some real, many imagined—of a frightening encounter with wild Apaches. Rumors continued to persist into the 1920s that remnants of Geronimo's band had slipped into the wilderness of the Mexican Sierra Madre and were still living the old ways, within striking distance of the border. Stan thrived on these eye-widening yarns spun by the cattlemen, ranch hands, and old-timers he encountered in the sparse ocotillo and mesquite-studded grasslands along the border.

The three amigos—Jones, Kendricks, and Hester—astride their big-eared burros, trundled east along the road known as the Geronimo Trail with their sights set on the Rogers Ranch. Nestled at the base of what is known today as D Hill, it was "Grandpa's Hill" to the boys. Hester's grandfather, George Rogers, and his brother John owned the ranch where the budding cowboys were gladly accepted whenever they wandered in on their dusty "broncs." Rogers, a veteran of World War I, was an exuberant storyteller who freely embellished the truth, a trait that Stan sopped up and exercised with unabashed skill as an adult. George fed the boys, entertained them with his tall tales, and assigned chores to perform around the ranch. It was at the Rogers Ranch that Stan "picked up an old guitar that had a split in it, and tried to pick out a tune. George Rogers noted his interest and gave him the old music piece."

Another neighbor, Levi "Capp" Watts, ran a few head of cattle north of D Hill. He supplemented his income by hiring out for other ranchers, and on the occasions he worked at the Rogers's place, he took a liking to young Stan. Watts was known by the nickname "Chap" before George Rogers insisted on calling him "Capp," which stuck for the remainder of his life. Often referred to as the "Old Hermit," Watts was best known locally for his uncanny talent for failing to ever rendezvous with a bar of soap. Born in Helena, Texas, just a year before the outbreak of the Civil War, Watts cowboyed his way across the Southwest. By 1889, he settled into work as a line rider for the Erie Cattle Company in Douglas, a large corporate outfit that paid him to keep Erie cattle out of Mexico along a thirty-five-mile length of the border that stretched across the width of the lower Sulphur Springs Valley. An extended drought in the early 1890s forced Erie to shift its operation to Kansas, but Watts stayed in Cochise County and homesteaded 160 acres in the Ash Springs area of the Perilla Mountains. Watts built a modest shack on his Ash Springs spread where, along with his small herd of cows, he wrangled horses that bore the genetics of Steel Dust, a horse born in Kentucky and renowned as the progenitor of the American Quarter Horse. Watts decided to sell his place in 1905 for $600 and moved to a dugout in the side of Saddlegap Mountain.

Ervin Bond, an amateur historian of Cochise County, recalled running across Watts and getting an unplanned tour of his primitive digs in 1926. Having recently arrived in Douglas, Bond headed toward Saddlegap Mountain as a hiking destination. After venturing up a steep ridge to survey the surrounding vista of the Chihuahuan desert, he began to bushwhack down a canyon to return to his vehicle. He came across a small spring with good water and stopped to drink and fill his canteen. He noticed the spring was tapped with a pipeline that ran down the canyon. Continuing on his way, he was startled by the sudden appearance of a "long-haired, bearded man on a rock within a few yards of my path." Watts, initially terse and suspicious, soon warmed up and offered to reveal his raffish domicile. Bond remembered:

> We walked to his home and I looked inside to see a bed made from lumber
> with some old canvas for a mattress, a small stove with a large pile of ashes
> in the rear. The smell of stench was so strong that I soon backed away
> without going inside for a better look.

Besides his reputation as a rather aromatic gent, Watts also gained notoriety for eschewing the use of a spoon or fork, choosing instead to sip his soup directly and noisily from the bowl, while using only a knife to shovel in his vittles.

Ervin Bond became a grocer in Douglas and recalled how Watts rode into town every other week atop his favorite horse, trailed by at least a half dozen more horses. Watts usually hitched his equine entourage behind the Gadsden Hotel and on every trip for six consecutive years, shopping sack thrown over his back, proceeded to give the exact same grocery list to Bond, who attended to Capp's shopping needs with a quiet smile.

It was Capp Watts who branded the vision of phantom cowboys chasing "red-eyed cows" across the stormy heavens into Stan's fledgling imagination. The apocryphal story persists that Watts invoked the "Ghost Riders" to quell young Stan's panic at the approach of a menacing thunderstorm as they serviced a windmill together on Capp's property. An article written by Ervin Bond in a 1972 *Cochise County Historical Society Journal* draws on his acquaintance with Watts in the 1920s and early 1930s to paint a colorful portrait of Capp's eccentric character and to spin how Stan first learned of the Ghost Riders. On Stan's handful of visits to Douglas as a famed songwriter during the 1950s, it's probable that he spoke with Ervin Bond, telling him a story or two of where and when Capp had first mentioned the Ghost Riders. What is improbable are the facts posited in Bond's 1972 fly-on-the-wall chronicle of what actually transpired between Capp and Stan back in the mid-1920s.

The "gospel" of the Ghost Riders according to Ervin Bond encompasses three separate instances that eventually drove home the visage of the phantom riders into the future songwriter's imagination. The first installment reads:

> It was around April of 1924 when Stan and three of his buddies rode out to where George Rogers and Capp Watts were about to drive a herd of cattle into a corral. The boys assisted in this chore and when it was finished Stan saw a big black cloud hanging just across the line in Mexico. Stan told his friends that they had better head back to town before it rained. Capp Watts spoke up and said, "Don't hurry son, that's just the Ghost Riders rounding up those clouds, after they get this done around July or August it will rain." Well as usual for southern Arizona it did not rain that April day, but neither did Stan see any Ghost Riders. However, he probably looked for them every time a cloud came up.

The second chapter of this drama unfolds with Stan out at Capp's little rancho about five months later. Bond writes:

> In September of 1924 Stan was helping Capp adjust and oil his windmill. A thunder and lightning storm came up suddenly and got so severe that they had to take refuge under some cliffs. Stan, just a boy of ten, told Capp he was afraid, to which the old Hermit replied, "Don't be afraid, it is only the clouds stampeding and the Ghost Riders will get them rounded up soon and everything will be alright." Again Stan searched for the strange riders, but he could not see them.

Finally after Stan has turned fourteen, he's awarded a glimpse of the elusive cloud wranglers:

> Four years later, on a Sunday afternoon, Stan was riding back to town from the Slaughter Ranch and as he reached "D" Hill he pulled his burro jack

to a halt. He could see storm clouds hanging low over the Sulphur Springs
Valley; as usual he looked for his ghostly riders and their herd, and this
time he could visualize them everywhere along the edges of the clouds.

Old windmills still dot the scrubby desert landscape east of Douglas along
the Geronimo Trail. Some have fallen into disrepair while many are still
twisting and creaking with the wind, drawing up water for cattle. It's entirely
feasible that Capp and Stan were indeed atop one, perhaps even on a windmill that still stands, when a savage storm blew in, driving them to seek shel-
ter and inciting Watts to share his "legend" with his nervous helper. There
are probably a few nuggets of truth glittering among Bond's embellished
renderings of Stan's original acquaintance with the Ghost Riders.

Capp Watts died in 1932 and is buried at the Calvary Cemetery in Douglas,
only a few hundred yards from the bronze plaque marking the grave of Stan
Jones. In the fall of 1991, the Cochise County Historical Society placed an
unpretentious new headstone at the gravesite of Watts. Under Capp's name
and the years of his birth and death, it reads: "An old cowpoke went riding
out one dark and windy day / He taught Stan Jones about Steel Dust horses
and Ghost Riders in the Sky." Stan had learned more than just a portentous
legend from Watts. Capp was the real McCoy: a stinky, hardened old cowpoke who weathered the transition from the nineteenth century frontier
into the modern, post–World War I era with his spurs and chaps intact. He
handed down his deep knowledge of old-time cowboy life and lore to the
eager, impressionable kid, who couldn't have cared less whether or not the
old hermit ever took a bath.[1]

   In a childhood bereft of his father's presence, Stan benefited from contact
with an eclectic array of paternal surrogates during those formative years. In
Clarence and Clara Hinton's household, Stan was in the presence of a young
man who had fought overseas in World War I and held a good job with
Phelps Dodge. When Clarence's father was on the premises, Mayor Hinton
afforded Stan the chance to enjoy largely unexaggerated reminiscences from
a man who had experienced the frontier West firsthand. Charlie Nichols fired
Stan's imagination with theatrical tableaus of Apache warriors, while lead-

---

[1] When Watts was struggling with his health toward the end of his life, he eventually landed in the
Cochise County Hospital, where Ervin Bond observed that Capp "seemed to enjoy being kept clean for
the first time in many years."

Stan with his mother Berta in Sonoma, California, 1947. *Courtesy of Bill Dubs*

ing the young scout into an enriching world of nature and woodcraft. The Reverend Simonson inspired Stan to "carry the cross." George Rogers taught Stan how to stretch a story, and put an old guitar in the young cowpoke's hands. Capp Watts revealed the trail that led Stan to the mythic lair of the Ghost Riders.

Although these men filled in admirably as substitute father figures, Stan never forgot to whom he owed the greatest debt of gratitude. Berta Jones had tolerated her son's wanderings of his hometown streets and beyond, out into the desert cow country where he absorbed the day-to-day tenor of ranch life and learned to rope and ride. She had also guided Stan to the brick edifice of St. Stephen's Episcopal Church where the doors of sound, practical religious instruction were opened to embed a lifelong spiritual grounding in her son. Although Berta would soon be tearing fourteen-year-old Stan away from the Arizona streets and ranchlands that he had grown to love, he would always remember that it was his doting single mother who struggled to maintain the two of them through tough economic trials. During Stan's scattered, often luckless attempts to stake a claim in the world after setting out on his own, he continued to carry the inspirational seeds planted in his spirit during those carefree, formative days in the Arizona borderlands.

As a gift to his mother a few years before he died, he inscribed on the cover of the sheet music to "Riders in the Sky (A Cowboy Legend)": "To Mom, who made this song possible 35 years ago. Love, Stan."

CHAPTER 3

IN THE NAVY

BY 1929, BERTA HAD DECIDED IT WAS TIME TO MIGRATE WITH FIFTEEN-year-old Stan to another one of her offspring's households and targeted her second-born, Nell. Nell Jones had left Douglas to attend nursing school in Alameda, California, around the time Stan was born in 1914. She was working at a medical center for returning soldiers in Petaluma, where she met and married Max Poehlmann. Situated in southern Sonoma County, Petaluma was an agricultural hub where rural goods from the region could be easily transported forty miles south to San Francisco via the Petaluma River and San Pablo Bay. Poehlmann was an early player in the thriving poultry industry in the handsome little farm town that would come to be known as "The World's Egg Basket."

Max tolerated his young brother-in-law's presence, but he and Stan were not particularly impressed with one another. Stan picked up a part-time job with a colleague of Max's, William Warner, who had a chick hatchery business. Stan would work for Warner on and off for the next five years during his sporadic visits to Petaluma.

Then Berta's youngest daughter Jeanne moved to Los Angeles to join a fellow from her Douglas neighborhood, William Dubs. They married there in 1927 and Dubs opened an auto mechanic business. By 1930, Stan and Berta had headed south to the Dubs's residence in Los Angeles to hitch their wagon to yet another family member. They were settled there long enough for Stan to complete his eighth-grade coursework, but the young cowboy's restless, freewheeling nature put him out on the road with his thumb in the air during the summer of 1931.

1932 Douglas High School 9th grade class photo. Stan Jones is standing at the upper left. *Courtesy of Cochise County Historical Society*

After several months of rambling, Stan landed back on Eighth Street with Clara and Clarence in September of 1931. Due to the unsettled wanderings of his mother, he had fallen behind a couple of grade levels. At seventeen, listing C. G. Hinton as his guardian, Stan began his ninth-grade studies at Douglas High School. Stan's hobo odyssey and his resulting creative efforts were featured front and center on the Woman's Page of the *Douglas Daily Dispatch* dated March 9, 1932:

Stanley Jones, But 17 Years of Age, Writes Manuscript Accepted by Youth's Companion

Stanley Jones, son of Mrs. B. M. Jones, of Los Angeles, who has been making his home here with his sister, Mrs. C. G. Hinton, has received word that a short story written by him will appear in a forthcoming issue of The Youth's Companion (American Boy) magazine.

The story is entitled "The Hitch-Hiker" and is about 10,000 words in length. Most of the story covers experiences which Stanley met with last summer during a hitchhike from Los Angeles to St. Louis, New Orleans and other points in the south. However, quite a bit of the story occurs in the southwest.

Interwoven with these experiences there is a bit of fictitious romance added by the author. He emphasizes the difficulties that arise on such trips and the moral of the story emphasizes the fact that boys should not attempt such trips because of the difficulties that arise.

Jones is but 17 years of age and this manuscript is the first to be submitted by him to a publishing company. The story will probably appear in an early summer issue of the magazine.

He attended high school here and in Los Angeles, and in addition to his literary ability, possesses a great enthusiasm for athletics. He was a member of the football squad last fall, and is interested in baseball and other sports.

Stanley has a collection of short stories on which he is working now, doing revision, and adding bits of human interest to make the stories more complete. As a general rule, he writes about the southwest, and is interested principally in nature.

He says there is nothing he enjoys more than to go into the mountains where there is no noise and remain there for hours, writing bits of short stories, formulating new plots, and rewriting some of his earlier manuscripts.

"The Hitch-Hiker" never appeared in the *Youth's Companion* and it's questionable whether Stan had journeyed all the way to New Orleans. This probably reflected an early stirring of Stan's propensity to spin the truth. It's notable that the *Douglas Daily Dispatch* does not mention that the teenager possessed any interest in songwriting. Stan's natural bent for songwriting surely sprang from the well of his family's deep love of music. At some juncture within the following decade, with a guitar in hand, he began to shape his creative urges into song.

It's unclear exactly how Stan passed the summer of 1932. Thanks to the work résumé that Stan provided to his Naval recruitment officers when he eventually enlisted in the military in the fall of 1934, there is a thumbnail sketch of his employment during the years prior to joining the Navy. He reported working on a milk truck in Douglas, perhaps helping out his old pal Wayne Hester. Stan had enrolled in a series of drama classes while in school and listed a stint performing with a "stock company on the road, acting." It's probable that the company staged hero/villain style western melodramas, giving Stan a chance to develop and showcase his musical talents during the olio variety show that commonly followed the main production.

By May of 1933, nineteen-year-old Stan had completed the tenth grade with a median standing in a class of 125 students. His conduct was considered "good" by the principal of Douglas High School, George A. Bergfield. Principal Bergfield recorded Stan's leaving school as "necessary employment." The local economy was anemic with the Great Depression in full stride, and Stan fell back, once again, on family connections. He journeyed to Petaluma to live with Max and Nell and labored in William Warner's chick hatchery. In the fall of 1933, he returned to Los Angeles to reunite with his mother and work as an occasional helper with Bill Dubs in his auto shop.

In the spring of 1934, with probable help from A. E. Hinton, Stan hooked up with a small gold mining operation on the American River in Placer County, California, not far from where the initial discovery of gold in 1848 at Sutter's Mill turned the history of the American West topsy-turvy. Max and Nell's son, Harold, remembers that as a boy of ten, he and his father visited Stan at the Big Bend Placer Mine. He recalls how his Uncle Stan and a couple of guys were working sluice boxes along the river, under which "little bits of gold would drop out." A character reference for Stan provided by the mine manager, Montgomery Westlake, to Navy recruiters a few months later states that the twenty-year-old young man was "quite sincere, courteous, and obliging."

By mid-August Stan was back in Petaluma, this time working for Max on his "chicken ranch," and neither Stan nor Max was happy about it. A grandson of Max's recalled his grandfather as "a pretty harsh dude." One of the older Jones boys, Jack, had served in the Navy, and at this juncture in his life Stan didn't have much to lose by swapping out his cowpoke bowlegs for a set of sea legs. He trooped into the Navy recruitment offices in San Francisco on August 23, 1934, writing on the application "none" when asked for a trade and entering "career" when asked the reason for his enlistment. He listed his home address as that of Max and Nell on Kentucky Street in Petaluma. When queried on the enlistment form whether or not his parents were divorced he answered "no." Stan wrote "yes" when asked if they were separated, echoing Berta's continued distress over the reality of the dissolution of her marriage almost two decades previously.

Navy recruitment officer C. W. Martin took stock of the five-foot-eight-inch, blue eyed, brown-haired, 151-pound Stanley Davis Jones, and recorded this estimate of the twenty-year-old recruit:

> JONES, Stanley Davis, is a lad of husky build, neat, well mannered, of average intelligence and I consider him good material for the Navy.

The mother keeps house for two sons and three daughters, all married, spends part of her time at each home.

The lad is of the type that I feel convinced would make good any where, as in these times of stress he manages to keep a job.

Dependency not likely.

During the Depression years, the question of whether a spouse or family member was dependent on a new recruit was a crucial determinant for selecting a future sailor, whose enlistment commitment was expected to last for four full years. At a starting salary of $21 a month, an apprentice seaman would be hard pressed to keep anyone else financially afloat. Still living in Los Angeles with Jeanne and Bill Dubs at the time of Stan's enlistment, Berta signed a notarized oath dated September 10, 1934, stating:

> I certify that I am not dependent upon my son for support, that he is not
> married and that he has never been married, that he has never attended
> any school having a correctional department and that I will not request his
> discharge from the Navy prior to the expiration of his enlistment.

The Naval recruitment process was also designed to weed out felons or juvenile offenders. Inquiries sent to the police chiefs of Douglas, Petaluma, and Los Angeles regarding Stan's past familiarity with any of their respective detention facilities came back negative. His employers' character references were all returned to the recruitment office with nary a discouraging word. William Warner of Petaluma proclaimed Stan's general intelligence to be "excellent" and his moral fitness and reputation in the community to be "very good." Bill Dubs gave a thumbs up to Stan as a trustworthy, capable, and industrious employee, adding, "All that I can say is he is a good boy and is fully up to all of the above standards." Max Poehlmann gave Stan positive marks across the board, but volunteered no additional hosannas beyond "yes" or "good" to the questions posed by the recruitment forms.

Stan Jones passed muster for entrance into the United States Navy and was officially listed as an apprentice seaman on December 15, 1934. Tagged on entry as possessing no remarkable skills and lacking training from trade schools, it was noted on his enlistment papers that "radio" might be the "branch of service for which best suited." His boyhood had provided him with at least one noteworthy skill on which he might hang his hat. He was immediately transferred to the United States Naval Training Station in San Diego, where his entry test marks were highest in "general classification," with a percentile rank of 85.5, and English ranked at 88.5. It's puzzling as to why he was not given the radio aptitude test that was listed but left blank on his report card. On all other categories, mechanical aptitude, arithmetic, spelling, and penmanship, Stan's score settled in the low fortieth percentile range.

He commenced his training regimen and orientation to the Navy but after six weeks landed in the U.S. Naval Hospital in San Diego with a diagnosed condition of "nervousness." Bill and Jeanne Dubs drove Berta from Los Angeles so she could visit with her beloved, bedridden son. He completed the treatment for his disorder successfully, returned to resume his military schooling by mid-March, and was promoted to seaman second class on April 21, 1935. Four days later, he marched up the gangplank of the USS *San Francisco*, a Navy heavy cruiser recently added to the U.S. Pacific Fleet, and Stan was seaborne, outwardly embarked on a glamorous four-year career to "see the world." The ship motored up the California coast and in June docked at the Naval Shipyard at Mare Island, near Vallejo, a relatively short distance from Petaluma. Stan was awarded five days of annual leave and spent some time at the Poehlmann residence.

Max and Nell's son, Keith, remembered his uncle's visit:

> He took me for a ride in my dad's big green Packard. We went up the steepest hill in Petaluma, which impressed the hell out of me since I had never been up or down it. When we got home I had to tell everyone about our adventure. Max was livid and there was a lot of shouting.

Somewhere along the line Stan became entangled with Helen Walsh, a student at the University of Washington in Seattle. It's not known if she was in the Bay Area while Stan was there on leave in June or if there was a whirlwind courtship at the ship's next stop at Puget Sound. Wherever he met her, Seaman Second Class Jones was a married man barely two months after his shore leave in Vallejo. Stan and Helen exchanged vows on August 17, 1935, at 4:15 p.m. on a Saturday afternoon before a justice of the peace in Kitsap County, home of the Puget Sound Naval Shipyard. The marriage certificate registered Helen Walsh as a resident of King County, Washington, and Stanley Davis Jones maintained his allegiance to Cochise County, Arizona. Stan reboarded the USS *San Francisco* soon thereafter and a few weeks later, on September 10, while the ship was docked at the San Pedro Naval Yard in Southern California, he assigned his new wife, Helen Walsh Jones, as the chief beneficiary of payments due resulting from his potential untimely demise while on duty. Her address, listed as 3521 Fifth Avenue, Los Angeles, California, is the same from which Stan's mother Berta made a desperate plea to the Navy one month later on October 11, writing that she is "very anxious to secure the release of my son" and is "not able to work and I need his help very badly."

In the midst of this new hubbub in Stan's personal life, he was transferred on September 19 via a hospital ship, the USS *Relief*, to the Naval Hospital at Mare Island, where he was, again, admitted for a nervous disorder. Stan spent the rest of his truncated Navy career at the Mare Island medical facility. Helen was clearly in cahoots with Berta, joining her efforts to spring Stan from his military obligations. From an address in Vallejo, Helen had also written a letter, pleading with the Navy for her husband's discharge. On October 7, 1935, Helen wrote:

> Dear Sirs,
>
> I am writing to your department in regard to my husband, Stanley Jones, who is a seaman second class in the navy.
>
> At the time of our marriage I was attending the University of Washington, and was not financially dependent on my husband. Since that time, however, unforeseen circumstances have arisen and I am totally dependent on him. Since his mother is also supported by him, we find it impossible to live on his income.
>
> Mr. Jones has a position awaiting him in Los Angeles, and we would be very grateful to know if there is any possible way for him to be discharged from the navy.
>
> Sincerely yours,
> Mrs. Stanley Jones

The U.S. Navy Board of Medical Survey recommended an honorable discharge and released Stan from his military duties on November 6, 1935, barely eleven months after his initial enlistment. Seaman Second Class Jones qualified for a Good Conduct Medal for his brief stay with the Navy, while at the same time was "not recommended for reenlistment." It's difficult to determine what weight the entreaties of Stan's wife and mother may have played in the Navy's decision to grant him a discharge. It's also open to question whether Stan was putting his theater experience to work to gain his release or if he possessed a genuine psychological disposition toward "nervousness" that made him truly unfit for service. Whichever the case, Stan Jones was a civilian once again.

A song that appears on Stan's 1957 Disney album, *Creakin' Leather*, suggests a budding songwriting effort by Stan during his short stint at sea on the USS *San Francisco*. The first reliable eyewitness testimony that puts a guitar in Stan's hands as he's belting out his self-penned "cowboy songs," comes from the mid-1940s. Although it's difficult to determine exactly when Stan turned to songwriting to express himself, the lyrics to "Deep Water" present tantalizing evidence that he was beginning to compose songs during his abbreviated hitch with the Navy.

"Deep Water" is a mysteriously atypical tune written by Stan, a black sheep amidst the flock of his customary cowboy-and-western themed songs that he excelled in composing throughout his career. Crooning a little like Elvis, he laments in the first two verses: "Deep water / So lies the harbor behind me / And all of the ties that bind me / To this lonely life I've known / Deep water / A gull winging home 'gainst the sundown / At last like the white gull, I found / You can never really leave home."

Here was a twenty-one-year-old landlubber who had likely savored one too many high sea adventure stories in *Youth's Companion* as a boy. Crammed into a slim berth in the bowels of a huge Navy cruiser, Stan, wracked with regret about his career choice, may very well have been pouring his heart out into verse. He had been married on August 17, and by September 19 he was on the hospital vessel that would carry him to Mare Island and his new wife, Helen. The final verse of the song envisions the blissful reunion that Stan pined for: "Deep water / The wake of the ship is her laughter / And all my tomorrows come after / I get back home to you."

CHAPTER 4

COWBOY, CHANGE YOUR WAYS

Stan's marriage to Helen Walsh signaled a fledgling effort on his part to settle down. But prior to that, while tagging along on his mother's nomadic wanderings, the randy young hombre had plenty of opportunities to get into trouble. Drawing on old-time cowboy vernacular, Stan had been cavalierly "stirrin' his stump." Just prior to his migration up to the placer mine on the American River in March of 1934, a frisky dalliance with a fifteen-year-old Mormon girl in Los Angeles had, unbeknownst to Stan, left her pregnant. The baby girl was carried to term, born in November, and immediately adopted by close friends of the girl's family.

There is evidence that Stan had left his mark in San Diego as well. The following letter from a woman named Patsy Fison was received by Naval officials on February 13, 1936. Dated February 4, 1936, it reads:

Dear Sirs,

I wonder if you could possibly give me any information as to the whereabouts of my half-brother, Stanley D. Jones, seaman 2nd class, last heard of in June '35 on the S.S. San Francisco San Pedro, Calif.

I am terribly worried about him as my last letter was sent from the San Francisco to the Relief ship to Mare Island Naval hospital and from there back to me. That was in Nov. '35.

I'll give you a description of him. He's 20 yrs. old, blond curly hair & blue eyes & very boyish looking.

I would appreciate it very much if you could tell me what ship he's on now and where he has gone. I remain,

Sincerely yours,
Miss Patsy Fison
Gen'l Del.
San Diego, Calif.

Ms. Fison added a postscript revealing her belief that Stan was still in the military: "P.S. He has been in the Navy approximately 16 months." The Navy replied in a letter dated February 18, 1936, that the "named man was discharged from the Naval service 6 November 1935." There is no evidence that Stan had a half-sister. Seaman 2nd class Jones presumably met Patsy out on the town during a ten-day leave from the previous April, 1935, while he was still at the Naval Training Station in San Diego. Stan shipped out April 26 on the USS *San Francisco*, and then proceeded to meet and marry Helen Walsh, leaving Ms. Fison, whatever her relation was to Stan, in the lurch.

By the mid-1930s, the Jones clan was not a close-knit family by any means. A rift between Jeanne and her older brothers Malcomb and Jack developed in 1927 when it was revealed that their father, John Edmond Jones, had entrusted a one thousand dollar insurance policy to his youngest daughter and left nothing to any of his other five children upon his death. Stan's brothers and sisters, scattered between Texas, Washington, and California, weren't particularly chummy with one another and most had lost track of their youngest brother. Stan saw Jeanne in Los Angeles and Nell in Petaluma, on occasion, largely because of his mother's continued dependence on them. A nephew of Stan's described him as "a lost sheep after the Navy—no one knew what he was up to."

Stan and Helen lived in Los Angeles for a time before they migrated up to San Francisco. A family member recalled: "Stan had an apartment there with his first wife near Golden Gate Park." In October 1936, their first child, Davis Walsh Jones, was born in Helen's hometown of Spokane, where her parents lived. A second child, Molly Anne Jones, was born in San Francisco in March 1938, but by the following year, Stan and Helen were divorced. The children remained with Helen while Stan cast about for his next move.

Once again, he relied on the generosity of family and made his way to Vancouver, Washington, where Clarence and Clara Hinton had recently relocated from Douglas. It simply isn't known exactly how Stan was employed during this period of his life. A number of thumbnail biographies of Stan put together in the late 1950s suggested that he worked for the Forest Service at one time as either a logger, firefighter, or snowplow operator. If indeed he had been engaged in any of these professions, it was during the years that he spent in the Pacific Northwest.

By September of 1939, Stan had married a woman named Kathryn Johnson from Vancouver, who was employed at the Swan Island Shipyard in Portland. Their daughter, Nancy Kay Jones, was born in 1941, but by the beginning of 1943 Stan was back on the loose. As the plaintiff in a divorce complaint filed with the Clark County Superior Court in January of that year, Stan attested·that he and his wife had "entered into this marriage hurriedly," that "they are not suited to each other," and "the attitude of mind of the defendant toward the plaintiff has been such as to constitute cruel and inhumane treatment." In the 1943 divorce decree, the court awarded Kathryn custody of Nancy as well as the household furnishings. Stan received the 1936 Ford Tudor sedan they owned and was ordered to pay ten dollars a month for child support.

Within a span of nine years, Stan had been married and divorced twice and fathered three children. Stan was learning the hard way that acting out of impulse was not a path that led to domestic bliss. The difficulty of finding gainful employment during the Great Depression had compounded the futility of Stan's attempts to establish a happy home. With World War II raging over two fronts, Stan looked once again to the military as a place to land. Perhaps acting on a forlorn urge to start over on the heels of his repeated lack of success at building a traditional family life, Stan attempted to reenlist in the Navy at the Portland Naval Recruiting Station. In a letter dated February 22, 1943, to the Bureau of Navy Personnel, he queried:

> I am writing you in regard to the status quo of my discharge on advisement of the local recruiting station. I wish to know whether I am eligible for induction into the Navy via my draft board; also may I be drafted or considered for such, due to the condition of my discharge.

If possible I would appreciate a rush on your reply as I am contemplating a change of occupation and residence in the very near future.

A reply from Navy Personnel arrived in early March, informing Stan of his eligibility through the Selective Service System to rejoin the military. If drafted, his future as a recycled sailor lay in the hands of the Armed Forces Induction Center, where he would be ordered to report. He decided not to test the judgment issued in 1935 by the Medical Board of Survey at Mare Island that he was "permanently unfit for service" and opted instead for "a change of occupation and residence."

World War II affected all aspects of civilian life in the United States. The American Red Cross led the charge to mobilize millions of volunteers across the nation to serve in understaffed hospitals, plant victory gardens, collect scrap, and to provide general assistance to the families whose loved ones fought overseas. Stan landed a supervisory position with the Deschutes County Chapter of the Red Cross in Bend, Oregon. Assigned as a Field Director at Camp Abbot, a combat training center for engineers, Stan was responsible for a range of services: managing volunteers who worked to facilitate communication between soldiers and their families, arranging for emergency financial aid to those in need, and distributing comfort articles and supplies that had been donated for the war effort. In Bend, Stan Jones met and fell in love with Olive Greaves.

Olive was a native of Preston, a small Mormon farm and ranch community located in the far southeastern corner of Idaho. Her father, Oliver, was known as a kind man with a wonderful sense of humor. Olive's mother, Katherine Greaves, also appreciated in the community for her mild-mannered kindness, taught for many years in a wood-heated, two-room schoolhouse. A cousin of Olive's shared, "In knowing her parents you can see where Olive acquired her sweet disposition and lovely manner." A popular, straight-A student at Preston High School, Olive, who was engaged in all school activities, was renowned for never saying "an unkind word about anyone" and being "a beautiful person, someone you were privileged to know."

Following in her mother's footsteps, Olive became a schoolteacher and was teaching in Bend when she met Stan that summer. Stan and Olive were wild about each other. Despite the turmoil of his past personal failures, Stan

Stan and Olive Jones. *Courtesy of Lynn Keller*

had retained his naturally bright, optimistic personality. A nephew praised his uncle's sunny countenance, declaring, "If you spent five minutes with my Uncle Stan, you'd have a friend for life." Olive was lovely, calm, and wholly accepting of Stan's effusive, outgoing disposition, while sharing his reverence for the wild open spaces of the West.

Stan Jones, at twenty-nine years old, had made a mess of his life thus far. Here was a chance for him to change his ways and set things straight. The tumbleweed trail that had led him from Douglas to Bend was littered with broken promises, fatherless children, and abandoned partners. The moral compass embedded in his heart from the teachings of the Reverend Simonson at the St. Stephen's of his youth hadn't been of much use for the restive adolescent. Adrift and lacking the guidance of a steady paternal hand while growing up, Stan had to figure out the rugged terrain of love and commitment on his own.

It's a mystery as to what exactly Stan had revealed to Olive before he asked for her hand in marriage. Many women might have fled for the hills upon learning about Stan's past performances as a husband. Despite what she may or may not have known about Stan's prior indiscretions and struggles with commitment, Olive trusted her instincts, said yes to Stanley Davis Jones, and gained a partner for life.

On New Year's Day, 1944, Stan and Olive were married at Camp Abbot by a United States Army chaplain. In July, the newlyweds transferred to Nevada where Stan took the reins of the Red Cross camp operation at the Fallon Navy installation. Sensing a need for invigorated entertainment op-portunities at the base, Stan spearheaded the formation of a theater group in October of 1944. Intending to include members of both the military and the local community, the troupe set out to take advantage of the "experienced makeup men, stage carpenters and other technical men at the base, as well as some talent." Stan's theatrical experience and vision for the inaugural play was disclosed by a front-page story in *The Fallon Eagle*:

> Jones, who has played in stock, and has had training as a dramatic director,
> will direct the productions, and said that the first to be attempted will
> be a melodrama of the gay nineties entitled "Pure as the Driven Snow, or
> the Working Girl's Secret," with a Dirty Dan for the villain and all the
> accompaniments of the robust theatrical favorites of the "days back when."
> He said that olio features will be prepared for between the acts, including a
> "can-can" chorus and barbershop quartets.

Just as the theater company started to gather steam, word reached Stan in December that there was a ranger position open at Washington's Mount Rainier National Park. The job was available only to military veterans, re-ferred to then as "ex-service eligibles," and Stan jumped at the chance. Here was an opportunity for him to land a job back in the woods, where he could utilize skills gleaned from his most memorable adventures as a youth—his days as a scout roaming the Chiricahua Mountains and his apprenticeship as a cowboy on the Rogers Ranch.

The future ranger's personal charisma and worth to the community were praised in *The Fallon Eagle* on the announcement of the naval station losing "one of its more valued members":

> During his stay here, he has made himself appreciated and well liked by all
> who came in contact with him, not only carrying out the standard func-
> tions of the Red Cross in aiding in securing emergency leave and financial
> help—but also in morale and recreational work.

The same article about Stan's transfer also reflected his knack for fabricating his past. An outlandish tale chronicling his Navy career and a supposed stint in Asia afterward read:

> No newcomer to Navy ways, Jones pulled a three-year hitch from 1933 to 1936, coming out with a PhM1c [Pharmacist's Mate First Class] rate. He was on the cruiser San Francisco, then skippered by Royal Ingersoll[1], at present the Commander of the Western Sea Frontier. He put in two years in the pig-boat (submarine) service, serving on the Narwhal and Nautilus.
>
> After his Navy discharge, he made his first acquaintance with Jap shells, putting in two years in China with the American Volunteer Group, as an ambulance driver and medical assistant. After getting a few ambulances blown out from beneath him, he was returned to the States suffering from shock and combat fatigue.

Perhaps Stan's exaggerations were simply meant to bolster his long-suffering self-esteem that took a hit during the years his mother struggled to find financial and family security for her young son. Stan played along with his mother's charade that John Jones was somehow still a part of the family, even long after his father's death. The good-looking kid with the sandy hair who had entranced his Douglas neighbors with spine-chilling ghost stories was still at it, employing his imaginative powers at will. Stan Jones was a storyteller: it was in his blood.

Olive appreciated her husband's natural calling and was proud of his efforts to employ his creative skills by organizing the theater company at the naval base. With her encouragement, Stan continued to draw on his fascination with the glory days of the Old West and wrote stories to submit to western pulp magazines. Thanks also to a prescient gift from Olive, a Martin O-17T tenor guitar, Stan began to work at transforming his cowboy stories into cowboy songs. By February of 1945, Stan and Olive Jones were bound for new, unforeseen horizons together at one of America's premier national parks.

---

[1] This is true. Royal Ingersoll was in fact the skipper of the USS *San Francisco* during the short time Stan was aboard and went on to become commander of the western fleet.

CHAPTER 5

MOUNT RAINIER

AS WORLD WAR II CONTINUED TO RAGE, OPERATING BUDGETS FOR THE national parks predictably took a backseat to the dollars needed to conduct the military effort. Wartime rationing limited the availability of both gasoline and tires, curtailing most leisure travel. Meager visitation to America's parklands reflected the austerity of the times. The ranger division at Mount Rainier was staffed to a bare minimum, but Stan got his foot in the door due to a district ranger's decision to take a three-year leave of absence to join the war effort as a member of the Coast Guard.

Mount Rainier, founded in 1899 by President William McKinley, is one of our nation's oldest national parks. Anchored dramatically by the 14,410-foot hulk of the dormant volcano that John Muir proclaimed as the "noblest" of Cascade Range peaks, it is a snowy wonderland replete with 365 square miles of glaciers, old-growth forests, and sub-alpine meadows. Picturesquely nestled at the southern base of the mountain, the facilities at Paradise, Washington, served as the focal point for visitors who swarmed the park during the mild summer months to ogle fields of wildflowers and marvel at the dramatic glaciers ringing Mount Rainier.

For much of the year, Paradise was buried in deep snow, with an average of 680 inches falling annually. Winter activities were limited to wilderness forays on skis and tromping around the slopes of the mountain on snowshoes. Clouds engulfed the mountain and the surrounding forests for practically the entire month of February in 1945.

Stan and Olive took advantage of some down time between Nevada and their new home at Mount Rainier with holiday visits to their respective families. The Joneses did not own a car at the time so they traveled by bus. Eighteen inches of snow lay on the ground when Stan and Olive arrived at park headquarters at Longmire on February 17. Up the road at Paradise there was nine feet. They moved their modest possessions into one of a handful of homey cedar-sided cabins that housed park staff and soon settled in to become popular and active members of the local community.

Stan Jones and the National Park Service constituted a nearly perfect match. Rangers of that era did it all, from mundane maintenance chores to dangerous rescues, relying on inner grit, horse sense, and dedication to duty as they confronted any task that might fall their way. Stan's diverse mix of blue-collar experience combined with his warm, open personality and love of the outdoors made him an ideal public servant. Stan did, however, have a rebellious streak, fostered during the free-ranging days of his youth, which led to occasionally dissonant relations with his Park Service superiors.

W. Ward Yeager, chief ranger at Mount Rainier, deftly negotiated a tangle of bureaucratic red tape in order to shift Stan from the American Red Cross to the National Park Service. Yeager journeyed to the Pierce County Seat at Tacoma for a day to obtain the work clearance and referral certificate necessary to complete the hiring of his new ranger. On February 19, Stan began work as a laborer, reporting to the Paradise District of the Protection Department until Yeager was able to get the final okay for his employment as a full-fledged Mount Rainier ranger. By March 19, 1945, Stan was official: "Stanley D. Jones was entered on duty as a Park Ranger and is assigned to the Longmire District."

Doug Evans, a Longmire resident from that era, fondly recalls that Stan was a "vivacious, outgoing, very personable guy with a perpetual broad grin" and was also "frequently amused and chuckling." Evans vividly remembers Stan's passion for his music and that "he loved to strum his guitar and sing cowboy songs," requiring only the slightest or even no encouragement to "drag out his guitar and perform." At one social gathering, after a couple of songs from Stan, the group began to politely disperse while Stan, undeterred, "simply sang and played on." Another park resident recalled Stan's occasional disappointment at the rejection slips that accumulated for his cowboy stories that he submitted to western-themed magazines.

A neighbor of Stan and Olive's, Lorraine Larson, remembers the quiet pondering of some members of the community at Olive's patient tolerance of her husband's exuberant personality and like-minded friends. Larson recalled that it wasn't unusual for the Joneses to host parties where alcohol was freely consumed. On one infamous occasion, a fire lookout, down from his solitary post on the mountain for a biweekly resupply of groceries and a little rest and recreation, got roaring drunk and threw up into a potted plant in Stan and Olive's living room. For good measure, he repeated the process in the bedroom. As he was being hauled away over a Good Samaritan's shoulder, his barf-splattered shoes slid off onto the road, where they were discovered the following morning.

Stan's first month on the job found him accompanying the Paradise District Ranger H. G. Bender on weekend patrols up the mountain to inspect ski trails, buildings, and telephone lines. On one trip, a summer's worth of neglected garbage was hauled from the inn by toboggan, stuffed into the Paradise Community Building's fireplace, and unceremoniously burned. Routine patrols of campgrounds and other outlying facilities were made when conditions permitted, but during the winter, road and trail patrols were necessarily limited, opening the door to an inordinate amount of the rangers' time engaged in the construction of rustic cedar signs.

These wooden signs, emblematic of the National Park Service's vast system of trails, were sturdy rectangular planks treated to withstand local weather conditions. The legends were carved into the wood with an electric router, and the sign was then bolted onto an upright post to mark trailheads, trail junctions, and the mileages between them. At Mount Rainier, the signs were made of western red cedar, impregnated with creosote and linseed oil designed to resist the ravages of the long, brutal, wet winters. The local black bear population threw a wrench into this strategy by chewing the signs up like so much cedar jerky, increasing the almost constant demand for replacements.

Stan must have imagined that he had wandered through the gates of sign-making hell. March of 1945, his first full month of duty, was marked by a report from Ward Yeager stating, "the rustic cedar sign construction has received the most attention during the month with a number of signs completed and others in various stages of completion." One ranger recalled the advantage of being trapped in the sign shop as providing "lots of indoor work by a warm wood-burning stove during cold miserable winter days." The long snowy months slogged on into May as Stan and his fellow rangers dutifully churned out cedar signs.

The late snow pack finally began to recede and by the beginning of June a relieved cadre of rangers escaped from the sign shop to inspect the park's trails and install the fresh stockpile of signs. A more critical task was to ensure that all fire extinguishers in the park were checked and refilled and that all fire hydrants and hoses were set to go at a moment's notice should a structural fire erupt. Preparations for fire suppression were paramount for the coming summer months, and all rangers were required to take a three-day fire suppression course to prepare for both structural and wildland fires. The roads to the remote eastern portions of the park were finally cleared of snow, and Stan journeyed with Chief Ranger Yeager for orientation to the White River District, located on the northeast flanks of Mount Rainier, and to the Ohanapecosh District in the southeastern corner of the park.

By now Ranger Jones was basically familiar with the park environs, and his checklist of duties expanded with the approach of longer days, milder temperatures, and increased numbers of visitors. Stan, valuable to the ranger division for his knowledge of stock animals, was tasked with the delivery of horses to outlying districts and the hauling of supplies by pack animals to the scattered fire lookouts perched above the dense forests at the base of the mountain. He assisted the park scientist with measuring glaciers, helped to cut and clear snags that had fallen in public areas, disposed of road-killed deer, worked at the Nisqually Entrance Station, and sharpened tools in the fire shed—a typical jack-of-all-trades regimen for National Park Service rangers of the day.

On June 22, Harry S. Truman paid a surprise wartime visit to Mount Rainier National Park, arranged by the president's political ally and friend, Mon Wallgren, the governor of Washington. Stan and fellow Longmire ranger Carl Tice served on the National Park Service team that escorted the presidential party from the Nisqually entrance. Arriving a little past noon, the president was officially welcomed to Mount Rainier by Park Superintendent John Preston. As the motorcade wound its way through Longmire, it paused briefly for the line of thrilled local residents to wave to the president.

The motorcade arrived at the Paradise Inn, still surrounded by snow. Truman bounded out of his vehicle, tossed a few snowballs, and then ceremoniously signed the guest register at a special outdoor table reserved for the occasion. The entourage moved indoors to the inn dining room, where lunch was served. A waitress on duty at the time remembered the parade of dignitaries emerging from the snow tunnel at the inn's entrance. The president, obviously pleased to be away from the Oval Office, spied a piano in the lobby and proceeded to serenade the group with a song or two before sitting down to eat. After lunch, Stan and his fellow rangers escorted the convoy back to the Nisqually entrance where it exited the park by mid-afternoon.

By all accounts, Truman thoroughly enjoyed his visit to Mount Rainier. At the time he had reason to be upbeat. Victory in Europe had been officially declared on May 8, and with the work on the atomic bomb coming to a climax, he may well have believed the war in the Pacific would also be over soon. Overjoyed by the news of the Allied victory in Europe, hordes of Pacific Northwest citizens were raring to travel again. By July, Chief Ranger Yeager was forced to deploy his slim ranger force with extended hours for patrolling all roads and trails of the now-busy park. In his monthly summary of ranger activities for July 1945, Yeager frankly addressed the accumulated pressures that had been placed on his staff by the war:

> From most of the Districts in the park there has been a burden, made more
> heavy as of the first of the month. Under Wartime cut backs a problem
> arose as to how so few men could do so much. The situation was made
> simple at the time by the curtailment of travel. Now, however, the problem
> is once again very eminent. We are attempting what is more nearly a peace
> time travel year with a meager protection force of the darkest war years.

To make matters worse, the Department of the Interior had imposed a mandatory cut in the rangers' workweek, which according to the chief ranger "was equivalent to the reduction of the protection force of four men. We can only carry on as best we can with reduced forces." Yeager's pluck was tested even further come August when extraordinary weather combined with the elimination of gas rationing. The joyous prospect of victory in Japan (the official surrender was August 15) caused visitors "to flock to the park in unprecedented numbers." By month's end, Yeager, with typically stoic ranger resolve, wrote: "The protection force, however, was able to furnish essential service to the public and maintain the forest fire program to an acceptable degree."

In September, a crisis of a more immediate nature took place. On the first day of the month, high on Sugar Loaf Ridge, north of Paradise Lodge, twin brothers out skiing with a friend tumbled over a steep slope and disappeared into a deep crevasse. The frantic friend skied as far as the snow lasted and then ran the rest of the way down the mountain to the Paradise Ranger Station to seek help. A rescue party of sixteen men was assembled that included Stan and all the rangers from the Longmire and Paradise Districts as well as a number of volunteers from the hotel company. The team finally accomplished the tricky rescue and hauled the brothers out by about 8 p.m. Both were in critical condition and were driven by Rangers Tice and Yeager to Madigan Hospital on the Fort Lewis army base in Tacoma. At the end of the month, Yeager reported that both boys were still in casts with severe but not critical back injuries.

September 2, Labor Day, turned out to be a record travel day for Mount Rainier, and Yeager calmly noted in his monthly report that it was fortunate that the skiing accident took place on the first of September instead of the holiday. Ranger Stan Jones spent most of Labor Day helping to direct traffic at Paradise—just another weekend in the life of a national park ranger.

The onslaught of summer visitors began to wane finally, and except for dealing with hectic crowds on the weekends, Stan and his fellow rangers could begin to concentrate on back-logged maintenance and repair projects, closing campgrounds, and boarding up buildings in preparation for the heavy snows of winter. Rangers patrolled the park boundaries during the October deer and bear hunting seasons. Stan got an opportunity to help manage some of the local wildlife when a black bear became a skosh too comfortable among the Longmire residences. The district ranger report for November tells the tale: "On the 10th of the month it was necessary to restrain the activities of a particularly bothersome bear. Not withstanding the lateness of the season, the animal became such a pest that it was determined that maybe a change of scenery would be beneficial to his well being. At this writing the bear should be in excellent health." Ranger Jones had the honor of splashing an identifying swath of yellow paint across the bear's back before it was summarily hauled off to more remote pastures.

The park was hammered by early, heavy snowfall in the month of November, prompting Chief Ranger Yeager to note, without irony, "Some preliminary work has been started on rustic cedar signs in the ranger's workshop." In December, Stan organized all the young employees and school kids of Longmire to go Christmas caroling. A member of this community choir recalls gathering in the back dining room of the National Park Inn to rehearse and that Stan wasn't comfortably adept at finding the proper pitch he was searching for on the piano. The young caroler surmised, "Stan had probably composed all of his cowboy songs by ear."

The post-war resumption of winter sports activities created a change in the Park's operations, with a shift in emphasis to keeping the road between Longmire and Paradise free of snow. Funds for that work were appropriated and the ranger staff engaged in patrolling the icy roads and managing the weekend crowds that swarmed to the open slopes and ski trails that surrounded Paradise. The rangers paid the requisite attention to the repair and installation of winter-use signs relative to tire chains, road conditions, avalanche areas, and trail markers.

By the end of January, the snow load on the buildings of the Park became dangerously heavy and work was begun to shovel them off. On into February, the snow continued to fall and Longmire District Ranger Albert D. Rose observed: "The snow conditions at the beginning of the month were far above normal. Ranger activities were confined, for the most part, to this 'sport' of shoveling roofs for several days."

In March 1946, Chief Ranger Yeager transferred to Colorado's Mesa Verde National Park as the Assistant Superintendent, and Rose stepped up to fill his shoes temporarily. This left Ranger Stanley D. Jones to assume the role of acting district ranger at Longmire. Stan filed the following observations for the one and only monthly report that he was responsible for during his tenure at Mount Rainier:

> Routine work was carried on during the month but was heavy toward signs to the number needed in the Paradise area, increased travel, road opening, etc.
>
> On several occasions during the month, snowfalls made the use of heavy equipment necessary for removal.
>
> All but four days during the month were overcast or partly so.
>
> The mean temperature for the month was normal being 37 degrees.
>
> Forty-three inches of snow remain on the ground at the months end compared with thirteen inches last year at this time.
>
> There have been many signs repaired, constructed, or otherwise handled in the ranger shop during the month.

Stan had been at Mount Rainier for a little over a year and had seen a lifetime's worth of snow and cedar signs. He longed for the open skies of the arid

Southwest and began to shop around for another park to ranger in. The new district ranger at Longmire, William Heckman, reported in July that a "Mrs. Jean M. Baunsgard, age 59, died on the Van Trump Trail near Comet Falls and was packed out by Rangers Jones, Behrens, Butler, and laborer Carnau." He then noted, "Park Ranger Stanley D. Jones received his assignment to Death Valley and will be leaving soon."

On August 3, Stan was awarded a farewell lap around the park to haul supplies over to the White River ranger station. On the following day, Stan and Olive bid goodbye to their Mount Rainier friends and to the spectacular mountain that loomed over the forested landscape. The somewhat forbidding name of their next park assignment didn't exactly inspire visions of greener pastures, but Stan was delighted to be headed back to the Southwest. Olive, ever faithful to her husband, girded herself for their next adventure together in the desert sands of Death Valley.

CHAPTER 6

A HOT, MISERABLE, GODFORSAKEN HOLE

DEATH VALLEY NATIONAL MONUMENT[1] HAD ALSO SUFFERED FROM A dearth of ranger personnel during the war. When the war ended, Superintendent Theodore R. Goodwin, with newly appropriated funds in hand, contacted all ten ex-service eligibles from a list he had received from the U.S. Employment Service, and only two declined to accept. Transfer of Ranger Stanley Jones from Mount Rainier National Park to Death Valley received approval on July 15, 1946, and Stan advised he would report for duty in early August. Still without a car, Stan and Olive traveled to the monument by bus after taking a break to visit family in Idaho and Northern California. By mid-August they arrived in Beatty, Nevada, a gateway town near the eastern boundary of the huge desert expanse.

If his intention was to flee long winters, Ranger Jones chose well. The legendary snowfall at Paradise, where as much as ninety-three feet had been recorded over one winter season, stood in stark contrast to the infamous heat of Death Valley, where the thermometer hit 134 degrees at Furnace Creek in July, 1913, the hottest temperature ever officially recorded on the planet.

Covering about the same landmass as the combined states of Delaware and Rhode Island, Death Valley encompasses five mountain ranges, the

---

[1] National parks are created by an act of Congress, national monuments by Presidential Proclamation. There is little significant difference between them other than in name. President Herbert Hoover established Death Valley National Monument on February 11, 1933, just a few weeks before he relinquished the Oval Office to Franklin D. Roosevelt. President Bill Clinton signed the bill that created Death Valley as a national park in October of 1994.

Wildrose summer headquarters. *Courtesy of the National Park Service*

salt-laden depths of Badwater at 282 feet below sea level, and the bristlecone pine-flecked heights of Telescope Peak at just over 11,000 feet. Access to the monument at that time was by oiled or dirt roads and fed into the 112-mile-long desert sink from roughly the four cardinal directions, all leading eventually to the geographic center of the valley at Furnace Creek Ranch. The Pacific Coast Borax Company, a pioneer mining concern, operated the tourist amenities at the ranch and at the Furnace Creek Inn a mile up the road. In 1927 the company had moved its main borax operations from Ryan, thirteen miles east of Furnace Creek, to Boron, located about 120 miles to the southwest in Kern County, California. The company had discovered another source of mineral wealth by extracting "gold" from the pockets of the tourists who flocked to Death Valley National Monument in burgeoning numbers after the end of World War II.

Monument headquarters, a hodgepodge of adobe, wood, and tin buildings constructed by the Civilian Conservation Corps (CCC) during the 1930s, was spread throughout Cow Creek, located at the base of a series of mineral encrusted mud hills about three miles north of the Ranch. This was the administrative base of operations for the National Park Service during the winter season from October through May.

The summer months were hot. When Furnace Creek was still a year-round working ranch to serve the needs of the borax mines back at the turn of the century, workers often lay out in irrigation ditches or covered themselves with wet burlap sacks in attempts to stay cool enough to sleep at night. During the heat of summer, chickens at Furnace Creek, as the tale goes, were fed shaved ice to keep them from laying hard-boiled eggs. By late May the overnight desert temperatures on the valley floor hovered between 80 and 90 degrees. To counteract the heat, the entire operation at Cow Creek was moved lock, stock, and barrel up to the Wildrose summer headquarters, where, at the relatively benign elevation of 4,100 feet, sleeping at night was almost bearable.

Overseeing this seasonal pilgrimage between Cow Creek and Wildrose every year was T. R. Goodwin, who served as an engineer at Sequoia National Park before being assigned to Death Valley in 1934. By 1937, he had acquired the title of superintendent and helped oversee the building of more than five hundred miles of roads in the monument. He supervised the Civilian Conservation Corps construction of ranger stations, restrooms, and campgrounds, guiding the operations of the monument through the tail end of the Great Depression and the lean war years. Goodwin, a no-nonsense manager, was not particularly easy to work for. Matt Ryan, a distinguished Death Valley ranger during much of Goodwin's long tenure as superintendent, had this observation:

> The Goodwin years were a challenge and inspiration for those who
> worked with him. We all knew his unwritten requirements of performance
> were impossible to attain, but his enthusiasm kept all of us "kickin and
> scratchin" to please him, because somehow he conveyed to us his determi-
> nation to share his love of Death Valley with everyone.

Superintendent Goodwin noted in his monthly summary of events for August 1946, "Ranger Stanley D. Jones arrived and reported for duty on the 16th." After arriving at Beatty in the relative cool of a midsummer evening at 3,300 feet elevation, the Joneses were met by monument staff. There they began the 59-mile journey down onto the vast sink of the valley floor, west through the Sand Dunes and Devil's Cornfield, up and over Emigrant Pass, finally dropping down into Wildrose Canyon and the summer headquarters. The temperature at Furnace Creek had topped out at 113 degrees that day, the exact average high temperature for the month of August. Entrapped by

Death Valley Superintendent T. R. Goodwin. *Courtesy of the National Park Service*

the surrounding mountain ranges, the summer heat had a relentless tendency to simmer on through the evening and early morning hours. Olive recalled the nighttime descent into Death Valley as entering a "hot, miserable, god-forsaken hole."

Her first impressions of the Wildrose Camp weren't as utterly hopeless, but after a week Olive Jones was still overcome with the sense of being in "desolate and lonely" environs. Summer headquarters, a ragtag collection of wood-sided tin-roofed huts set along an open canyon bottom, was cloistered among smooth sagebrush hills with no remarkable vistas in any direction other than the distant panorama to the east, the high piñon and juniper dotted ridges of the Panamint Mountains. Thrilled to be back in an arid setting and chipper as always, Stan assured his wife, "Don't worry Ollie, wait until you get sand in your shoes, you'll learn to love this desert."

Ranger Jones was immediately put to work clearing the thick willow stands that choked the roadsides in Wildrose Canyon to ease access to the three springs between summer headquarters and Wildrose Station. About a mile down the road, Wildrose Station, an unpretentious, cottonwood-shaded resort, included a single gas pump, café and bar, and a handful of rustic cabins. The structures were tucked along both sides of the narrow canyon where a rugged dirt track led southwest down into the Panamint Valley. The small resort, closed during the war years, had recently opened for business with new owners and proprietors, George and Ann Pipkin. George Pipkin, journalist, Inyo County Deputy Sheriff, entrepreneur, and desert bon vivant, knew everybody in the Death Valley region. Ann Pipkin entertained Wildrose Station guests in the evenings with her guitar, soaring voice, and homespun songs about the desert that she and her husband loved with a passion.

When Stan got wind of an establishment just down canyon where he could enjoy a beer and perhaps warble a song or two, he cajoled his wife into walking down the road one evening. Encountering three rattlesnakes along the way did nothing to brighten Olive's mood, but they were embraced at once by the Pipkins as newfound friends and the Joneses quickly began to feel at home. Ann Pipkin, known as "The Songbird of Wildrose," and Stan discovered that they were musical soul mates, and before long the two were singing and playing guitars together under the cottonwoods and stars in a scene that would be repeated many times over during Stan's years in Death Valley.

Assigned to the Emigrant Ranger Station that same month, Stan and Olive Jones moved into the stone dwelling that they would call home for the length of their tenure in Death Valley. Built by the Civilian Conservation Corps in the late 1930s, the station was located approximately halfway between Cow Creek and summer headquarters at the junction of California Highway 190 and the road to Wildrose Canyon. The facade faced the highway, the main route visitors traveled to enter the monument from the Owens Valley. Intrepid drivers faced a serious chug up to 5,000 feet at Townes Pass from the depths of the Panamint Valley before plunging down the narrow road that wound through a steep boulder-strewn expanse. After eight miles, they arrived at the small cluster of rock buildings at Emigrant crowned by an American flag atop a tall pole that marked the official entrance into Death Valley National Monument.

The ranger station featured two doors, inset from the overhang of the front porch that was supported by four thick stone and mortar columns, leading, respectively, into a small room that served as the official Park Service contact office and into the ranger's living quarters. An alternate door on

Death Valley ranger Stan Jones at Wildrose Station. *Courtesy of Margaret Brush*

the western end served as the main entry into the unpretentious domicile, a few steps from the space where Stan parked his patrol vehicle, a 1942 Ford pickup truck.[2] Water was piped down canyon about four miles from Emigrant Spring to the ranger station, and a generator in a shed out back supplied electricity as needed. The primitive communication system consisted solely of two-way radio units in Stan's patrol truck and the ranger's office.

The remote setting at Emigrant suited Stan and Olive's shared streak of independence. They preferred to avoid mingling with the superintendent and other park officials headquartered at Cow Creek and soon developed a network of friends, mainly miners and ranchers from areas adjacent to the monument. The Stovepipe Wells Hotel, with accommodations for

---

[2] A truck commonly used by Federal land agencies in the 1940s. This was the last pickup model to roll off the Ford assembly lines before being retrofitted to produce tanks for the war effort.

eighty guests, sported a restaurant, tap room, gift shop, and service station. Only nine miles down Highway 190 from Emigrant, Stovepipe was a welcome venue in which Stan could entertain visitors and locals with his song-writing talents. Ranger Jones also assisted the park naturalist in presenting lecture programs about the natural history of Death Valley at both Stovepipe Wells and the Furnace Creek Inn. At the tail end of his talks, he invariably picked up his guitar to treat the visitors to a few of his "cowboy songs." When Stan and Olive did venture to Cow Creek, it was usually for the Saturday night square dances that were held on Chief Naturalist Floyd Keller's front lawn. There, Stan entertained the group with his talents during dance intermissions.

Ranger Jones spent his energies on the job as duty called. Stan roamed the vast desert monument in his patrol pickup, equipped with full canteens, maps, blankets, shovels, rope, chains, spyglass, smudge flares, flashlight lantern, first aid kit, and a lever-action rifle. He was at the ready to dig out vehicles stuck in the sand, cool overheated radiators, pursue lawbreakers, search for lost hikers, or simply to be a friendly, knowledgeable contact to the visiting public. Superintendent Goodwin, upon his return to the monument in October after a long vacation break, wrote in his monthly missive to the regional director that he was gratified to receive "very favorable reports" about his new Emigrant ranger. He also recorded that "fifty-one burros were disposed of during the month."

The controversial burro eradication program had been implemented at the monument since 1939. Burros abandoned by prospectors during previous decades had multiplied like so many rabbits, freely roaming the surrounding mountain ranges by the thousands. The hardy beasts, with no natural predators to keep their numbers in check, usurped forage and natural water sources, muscling out the fragile desert bighorn sheep populations, whose numbers had already been decimated by hungry miners. In order to honor the mandated goals of protecting native plants and animals within the national park system, T. R. Goodwin had instituted the policy of managing the monument's rampant burro population by "direct reduction," a bureaucratic euphemism for shooting the animals on sight. Rangers were expected to be earnestly involved in implementing the order, and this was one assigned task that Stan refused to carry out, much to the consternation of the superintendent.

Ranger Jones would just as soon destroy his guitar or stop singing than he would shoot any of the four-legged friends of his Douglas youth. Instead,

Stan with his ranger gear. *Allan Grant / The LIFE Picture Collection / Getty Images*

he was moved to write a tender, lilting composition he named "The Burro Lullaby." According to Olive, he wrote it exactly as the scene had unfolded. On the way back home from patrol one evening, Stan pulled his NPS pickup off to the side of the highway to enjoy a colorful Death Valley sunset and a twilight smoke. Hearing a stony clatter in the desert behind him, he turned to marvel as four burros, one at a time, stuck their big-eared heads up and came into view over a nearby ridge, gifting Stan with the inspiration for a song that begins with these lines: "One little burro on a hill, with evening comin' on / Two little burros on a hill, their shadows almost gone / Three little burros on a hill, beneath a purple sky / Four little burros on a hill, and they sang this lullaby." Stan began singing the song in public every chance he got and it quickly became a popular addition to his repertoire. This did not curry any additional favor for Ranger Jones with T. R. Goodwin.

Stan diligently carried on with his daily patrol duties, attempting to cover as much territory as possible throughout the tremendous expanse of Death Valley. A visiting wag remarked after a naturalist's program that had invoked some of the grisly handles for local geographic landmarks—the Funeral Mountains, Hell's Gate, and Coffin Peak—that the seldom seen ranger forces be dubbed the "Death Valley Skeleton Crew." Even with the post-war addition of personnel, it was nearly impossible for rangers to establish a meaningful presence at any one locale within the two-million-acre national monument.

In addition to lack of staff, an inordinate number of vehicle accidents plagued the hard-pressed rangers. Most roads leading into the Valley were deceptively steep, and Highway 190, careening sharply down toward the Emigrant Ranger Station from Townes Pass, was especially treacherous. The following report typified the range of vehicular mishaps that Stan might happen upon at any time of the day or night:

> An accident on Highway #190 above Emigrant Ranger Station which
> involved the neglect of a warning "dip" sign, caused the machine driven
> by Mr. H. P. Rogers of Burbank, California, to travel seventy feet in the
> air from the point of take-off before coming to earth and then rolling and
> coming to rest eighty yards from the dip on its wheels. Both Mr. and Mrs.
> Rogers ending up in the back seat, the cushion resting on their heads.
> Fortunately the only injury suffered was by Mrs. Rogers receiving a dislo-
> cated shoulder.

Visitation to Death Valley usually peaked during the spring months and rangers were expected to keep visitors apprised of park policies. Ample winter rainfall had produced the expectations of a spectacular spring wildflower display. By February of 1947, a flood of visitors began to pour into the monument, prompting T. R. Goodwin to sternly observe that "many persons violating Park Service regulations against the picking of and taking away of natural flora were informed of the regulations and warned against further violations." Stan simply advised any floral-snatching scofflaws that he ran across to "please don't pick the flowers."

Aside from his day-to-day contacts with the visiting public, Ranger Jones could be found breaking up fights between drunks at Stovepipe Wells, taking the daily weather readings at Cow Creek, helping set a large white cross at the Sand Dunes for Easter Sunrise Services, or refilling water barrels placed strategically along the monument roads to help cool overheated radiators. These were the salad days for NPS rangers when there was no specialization of duties as there is today; a ranger's responsibilities ran the gamut from cleaning out toilets at the comfort stations to lugging bodies of unfortunate hikers out of the backcountry.

One winter day, Stan and his deputy sheriff pal, George Pipkin, were driving around the back roads of the Panamints in Pipkin's Army-surplus jeep, when they came across a local out-of-work miner illegally scavenging some machinery from the old Skidoo gold mill. Figuring he could outrun Pipkin's weathered old clunker, the miner gunned his truck and hightailed it for the Emigrant Canyon Road as the ranger and the deputy bounced along in earnest yet feeble pursuit. Once the villain reached Highway 190, he raced away downhill toward Furnace Creek. When Stan and George finally reached the Emigrant Ranger Station, Ranger Jones jumped into his patrol truck, picked up the trail, and finally nabbed the offender at the Furnace Creek Ranch. The miner was hauled off to the county seat in Independence, where, according to George Pipkin, he was sentenced to a six-month jail term. This was a fortuitous outcome, considering the offender's current state of affairs, as it was the middle of winter, he was unemployed, and he was happy to get three squares and a warm bunk.

Stan's innate bravura was put to the test a few days before Christmas in 1947. He happened to be chatting with Chief Ranger Ted Ogston in his office at Cow Creek when a frantic gentleman squealed his car to a stop out front, rushed into the headquarters office, and blurted out that his son had slipped while attempting to climb up the unstable gravel slopes of a canyon in the Black Mountains. The three men jumped into Ogston's patrol vehicle and roared down the Badwater Road to Natural Bridge Canyon, where the boy, scared and stranded on a precipitous ridge of crumbly mud and rock, clung to a narrow perch. George Pipkin's breathless account of the rescue reads:

> When they reached the scene of the accident, Ranger Jones kicked off his boots and began to look for a way to start the climb up the sheer wall. There wasn't any. It was impossible for him to climb directly up to the 17 year old youth, he had to work his way around to gain the top of the hog-back above him, then work down toward the youth. The going was tough. Working down to a razor sharp ridge he came to a crevice. Only way to get over it

Winter headquarters at Cow Creek. *Courtesy of the National Park Service*

was to jump. If he made it, he would have to land on his knees and maintain a balance. If he didn't make it he would be a goner. As he sat weighing
the chances, he could hear the injured youth moaning and he could see one
of his hands grasping the side of the crevice. Time was running out. Any
moment the boy might lose his grip and plunge 150 feet to instant death on
the rocks below. Jones jumped, landing on his knees, he felt himself going
off balance; there was nothing to hold on to, just the pressure of his knees
on the hog-back. The moment that it took for him to regain his balance
seemed like an eternity. Working downward to the youth, he could only
get within twenty feet of him. Resting a moment, he asked the youth if he
could use his arms. He was more scared than injured. Jonesy tossed him the
rope and instructed him to slip his arms into the loops, like putting a vest
on backwards, and to put his belt through a loop, also a foot into another
loop. When this was done, he began in a confident voice to talk the youth
up the slope. "Relax, take it easy and start climbing as I pull; whatever you
do don't look down. If you slip you'll only fall far enough to think that the
rope has cut you in two. Steady, boy, now come on."

With Ogston's shouted guidance from below, Stan and the boy eventually
negotiated their way to the bottom of the canyon, and the young fellow's

parents were overcome with relief and gratitude. Stan's bloody and bruised feet were exposed as the socks he had on at the beginning of the rescue were now tattered beyond repair.

The father, struggling for a way to thank the valiant ranger, instinctively offered him money. Stan brushed this off curtly with an "all in a day's work" shrug of his shoulders. The boy's mother offered to send Stan a new pair of socks and he also declined this offer, telling the woman thanks, but that his wife had knitted them for him as a gift and that they were irreplaceable. George Pipkin describes the conclusion of the rescue scenario: "As he and Ogston walked away her voice trailed after him saying she would send some yarn." Superintendent Goodwin's report of the incident was characteristically more matter of fact: "Ranger Jones made the climb in his stocking feet, something that would have been impossible for the Chief Ranger to do."

On mild evenings the Joneses often enjoyed a picnic in the sand dunes and then they would swing by Stovepipe Wells afterwards to visit local acquaintances and to give Stan a chance to sing and play for the hotel guests. George Palmer Putnam, a good friend and stalwart fan of Stan's musical talents, owned the Stovepipe Resort. A scion of the wealthy G.P. Putnam Sons publishing empire, Putnam had been married to Amelia Earhart at the time of her disappearance over the Pacific in 1937. In 1940, the driven and hardworking writer, explorer, politician, publisher, and lecturer had found a wilderness refuge in Inyo County at Whitney Portal, perched at an elevation of 10,000 feet in the Eastern Sierra. With the onset of World War II, he applied at the age of fifty-five for a commission as an intelligence officer with the Army Air Corps, served in the Asian Theater, and then in 1945 returned to his high-altitude sanctuary in relatively poor health. Major Putnam had remarried, and his new wife Peg quickly discovered she preferred the gentler desert climes of Inyo County at sea level during the frigid Sierra winters.[3] The Putnams began treating Stovepipe Wells as a second home, prompting George to buy the place outright as a gift for Peg when it was for sale in 1947. Although a friend and admirer of T. R. Goodwin, the major didn't think much of the burro reduction campaign and was often found in the Stovepipe bar, harmonizing along with Stan on a soulful version of "The Burro Lullaby."

---

[3] Inyo County, the second largest in California, ranges over 10,000 square miles. It contains both Mount Whitney, the highest peak in the continental United States at 14,505 feet, and Badwater, the lowest point in the western hemisphere, 282 feet below sea level, in Death Valley.

Olive Jones passed the days quietly knitting or reading in the cozy ranger's living quarters that she had spruced up with framed pictures, collectible plates, a cuckoo clock, and a knitted afghan draped over the back of a small sofa. One Christmas season she helped out the Borax Company's hotel operation by working at the front desk of the Furnace Creek Inn, but found she preferred the solitude at Emigrant. With Stan usually away on patrol for much of the day, Olive would greet visitors who stopped in at the ranger station, pass out maps and pamphlets, and in her patient, kind demeanor, answer any questions they might have about what to expect "down there" in the desolate salton sink of Death Valley.

Early one evening, a gnarled prospector plodded down the highway toward Emigrant, trailed by a couple of pack-laden burros, and was entreated by Stan to stay for supper. Olive privately observed that "he looked like he hadn't combed his hair in thirty years" and then went into the small kitchen to prepare something to eat. Stan soon stuck his head in the doorway loudly whispering, "Hey Ollie! Have we got any soup? He doesn't have any teeth!" After a modest dinner of soup their guest was offered the use of a cot for the night. "No," he responded crankily, "I'll just sleep out on the ground with my burros, like I always do—I wouldn't want to coddle myself." Recounting this story so many years later, Olive was still tickled by the old codger's use of the word "coddle."

On another occasion, an elegantly attired woman traveling alone stopped at the Emigrant Ranger Station early one afternoon. She had decided to detour through Death Valley on the way back from her southwestern travels to her home in San Francisco. Discovering that Olive was by herself out in what the city-bred traveler perceived as the absolute middle of nowhere, she blurted out, "How can you stand living out here?" Olive smiled and gently engaged the woman's curiosity, describing her rural background and the life that she and her husband had forged together, choosing to live and work in the natural splendor of western national parks. This mollified the woman, who relaxed and accepted Olive's offer of a chair on the front porch. They sat together, sharing their individual stories while gazing out across the dark boulder-strewn alluvial fan that surged down toward the vast northern expanse of Death Valley. Suddenly conscious that a couple of hours had somehow passed, the woman figured that she had best get back on the road. She expressed her pleasure at having met Olive and parted with an assuring nod, "I understand now why you love it here."

Stan and Olive Jones at Wildrose Station. *Courtesy of Myrtle Murchison*

The nighttime skies glittered brilliantly over the Jones's stone abode. A lost, gold-seeking pioneer who had trekked across Death Valley in 1849 aptly depicted the glowing firmament, where "no stars forgot to shine." Stan and Olive reveled in the peace afforded by their humble quarters with sweeping views of the desert that Olive, indeed, had come to love. "My husband was right," she mused during an interview nearly sixty years later, "I did get sand in my shoes."

CHAPTER 7

NO WATER IN THAT CACTUS

STAN CONTINUED TO WRITE SONGS WHEN THE SPIRIT MOVED HIM, usually while propped up in a chair with his tenor guitar on his front porch. Besides "The Burro Lullaby," he wrote two of his finest songs in Death Valley: "Cowpoke" and the immortal "Ghost Riders in the Sky." Margaret Brush, the daughter of George and Ann Pipkin, remembers spending weekends at Wildrose Station as a teenager, listening to her mother and Stan playing and singing "Ghost Riders" together. She recollects that this was in 1947, the year that Stan likely wrote his iconic song. For Ranger Jones, "Ghost Riders" was just one of a handful of tunes that he had composed while living in Death Valley and there was no reason to whoop and holler about the specific day that he had written the song—not yet anyway. When he carved "Riders in the Sky 6/5/48" onto the face of his guitar sometime in 1950, it was to commemorate more than just his thirty-fourth birthday. It was to mark the date of a decisive turn of events in the Singing Ranger's fortunes.

In May of 1948, Hollywood converged on Death Valley. The spectacular, austere desert landscape had been used for location shoots since the pioneer days of the film industry. Under the heading of "General Publicity" in his May Superintendent's Report, T. R. Goodwin wrote:

> The three movie picture companies, Twentieth Century Fox, Argosy
> Pictures, and Columbia Pictures, with combined personnel numbering

342, leased the Furnace Creek Ranch and Stovepipe Wells Hotel company
facilities for the greater part of the month.

On May 3, the Furnace Creek Ranch was closed to the public to make way
for director John Ford and a cast and crew numbering more than one hundred to shoot a film titled *3 Godfathers*. Written as an allegorical twist of the
biblical three wise men tale, the story was also the basis for a 1919 silent film
directed by John Ford called *Marked Men,* which starred Harry Carey Sr.
The film *3 Godfathers* is the story of bank robbers on the lam who adopt a
baby boy they are shamed into delivering when they find his dying mother
stranded in a broken-down covered wagon. The leading roles were played by
John Wayne; Ward Bond; Mexico's top box office draw, Pedro Armendáriz;
and Harry Carey Jr. Nicknamed Dobe by his father the night of his birth for
the shock of mud-colored hair at the top of his noggin, Carey Jr. preferred
this moniker, especially after the worldwide notoriety of the desperate "hari-
kari" Japanese suicide bombers near the close of World War II.

One of the most important American film directors of the twentieth century, John Ford was a complex, difficult, and often sadistic man who, much
like Swedish filmmaker Ingmar Bergman, tended to work with a familiar
stable of actors and actresses who knew and accepted his human foibles.
Harry Carey Sr. had recently died, and despite a tempestuous relationship
with him, Ford dedicated *3 Godfathers* to his old friend's memory and invited Carey's son to co-star in the film. Although Ford insisted that Carey
call him "Uncle Jack," the young actor was nonetheless petrified at the idea
of working for the first time with the demanding director. Ford warned him,
"You're going to hate me when this movie is over, but you're going to give a
great performance."

Ford not only imposed a tight dictatorial command of his film sets, he
also tended to control the leisure activities of his leading men. John Ford
loved his liquor, but booze was off limits for all cast members, including the
director himself, while on location. Instead of drinking, Ward Bond, John
Wayne, and Pedro Armendáriz would gather at Ford's behest every evening
at the Furnace Creek Ranch to play dominoes. In typical Ford fashion, he
assigned the rookie Carey the role of "water boy," requiring him to keep
the keenly competitive domino players supplied with glasses of iced mineral water. This gave Dobe the opportunity to quietly observe that Uncle
Jack cheated at every opportunity. In an excellent memoir by Carey, entitled *Company Of Heroes,* he recalls in candid detail the verbal sparring and

Publicity still from *3 Godfathers:* From left to right, Pedro Armendáriz, John Wayne, and Harry Carey, Jr. *Courtesy of Lone Pine Film History Museum*

obscene zingers that flew between the "Old Man" and his star actors. One evening, Wayne suggested to Armendáriz that perhaps they should let Ford win at dominoes with the hope that "he might be nicer the next day."

Ward Bond's role in the film was the sheriff, Pearly Sweet, with whom a ragged posse gallops all over the badlands of Death Valley in pursuit of the three bank robbers. Not blessed with as much screen time as the other main players, Bond and his "deputized" team of bit players would while away most days up at the Furnace Creek Inn swimming pool, awaiting the "call" from the Old Man. In an eerie foreshadowing of the role Eden Ahbez, composer of "Nature Boy," would eventually play in ushering "Ghost Riders in the Sky" onto the American airwaves, Carey recalled clearly Ward Bond's obsession with the popular song that was high on the Hit Parade charts that spring:

> Nat King Cole had a big hit record out while we were filming, called "Nature Boy." Ward sang it all day long. I am sure Ward thought that he sang it better than Nat, but he sang it in the style of Louis Armstrong. He actually did a pretty good rendition. Hearing that song always makes me feel like I'm back in Death Valley.

Modern movie companies are notorious for giving the regulations of national parks and other federal land agencies short shrift in their myopic, oftentimes frantic, quest to get "the shot." The National Park Service, exercising its public mandate to "preserve and protect" all of the cultural and natural resources within its borders, has a rigorous permit process that specifically spells out the acceptable boundaries that a film crew must stay within.[1]

The NPS regulatory grip wasn't quite as rigid back in the 1940s, and John Ford's love of the dramatic Death Valley vistas are reflected in the finished color film that is loaded with repeatedly stunning footage shot throughout the area. Nonetheless, Superintendent Goodwin made sure that a park ranger was on board at all locations to "check on any violations of Park Service rules." Most of the "chase" scenes from *3 Godfathers* were filmed near Zabriskie Point, Natural Bridge Canyon, and out on the valley floor. The latter part of the film where "Bob, William, and Pedro" (Wayne, Carey, and Armendáriz respectively) become godfathers was played out in the sand dunes, a mere raven's glide away from Stan's stomping grounds in the vicinity of Stovepipe Wells.

Ranger Jones was on hand for a scene set in the sand dunes on a day in which John Wayne hacked into a barrel cactus with a machete to obtain water for the newborn baby and the thirst-crazed godfathers. With cameras rolling, Wayne squeezed the chunky cactus pulp without a drop of moisture finding its way into the canteen held by Dobe Carey. Unaware of John Ford's disci-

---

[1] One notable example of a company's egregious disregard for the rules occurred during the filming of a scene in the East Mojave for Oliver Stone's *The Doors* in 1990. A surreptitious eleventh-hour change in the agreed-upon color medium used to paint ersatz Indian pictographs on the pristine walls of a limestone cavern were in fact not "removable" as originally promised, fueling the outrage of desert lovers who believed that Hollywood should not be allowed in the wilderness.

plinary demeanor on his movie sets, Stan, in his typically relaxed and breezy manner, piped up, "You can't get any water out of that kind of cactus!"

Ford, unaccustomed to being interrupted in the middle of shooting a scene, yelled "Cut!" and tensed like an angry pit bull. He slowly turned in his chair and barked, "Who the hell said that?" Ranger Jones, unfazed, stepped forward. "I did, Mr. Ford. That barrelhead cactus has some moisture in it but you'll never get it to drip into that canteen." "Who in the hell are you?" Ford demanded, "and what makes you a goddamn authority on cactus?" "It's my job, sir," replied Stan, resplendent in his Park Service uniform and flat hat, "No water in that cactus."

Ford had a crewmember soak the chunk of barrel cactus overnight in a bucket of water, and the following day, bolstered by a hidden sponge for backup, shot the scene with plenty of water to drip into the canteen. Satisfied with the effort, the director yelled, "Where in the hell is that ranger who said there wasn't any water in that cactus?" Stan, off smoking a Camel at the back of the set, came forward, and Ford had Wayne and Carey retake the scene for Stan's benefit. "Did you see that Jones? There's water in that goddamn cactus. You told me yesterday there wasn't any." Stan laughed it off, not realizing, and probably not caring, that he had earned the begrudged respect of the famous director. Stan drove home to Emigrant each evening after the day's shoot, while Ford's company headed thirteen miles south to their base at Furnace Creek. It would take better than a year for John Ford to get the opportunity to appreciate the gutsy ranger's natural songwriting talents and offer him a job.

By May 19, 1948, Ford and his team had wrapped up their efforts in Death Valley, earning accolades from T. R. Goodwin in his monthly report for May: "The behavior of the crew was perfect throughout their stay. They were favored with perfect weather throughout and did not lose an hour." Overlapping with Ford's RKO Studios endeavor was the Columbia Pictures crew that arrived on May 10 to shoot a movie entitled *The Walking Hills*. Half of the 120 crewmembers took over the Stovepipe Wells Hotel facilities, and the remaining personnel took up residence on the premises in a temporary tent camp. Directed by John Sturges, the film revolved around a diverse band of modern gold seekers trying to locate a treasure-laden wagon train buried by shifting sands one hundred years before, who begin to turn on each other as the harsh elements intrude on their quest for easy riches.

George Palmer Putnam personally escorted the producer of the film, Harry Joe Brown, through the desert surrounding Stovepipe, and Brown

Courtesy of the author

remarked, "Major Putnam has shown me lots of grand location places in and around Death Valley. It's a remarkably rich field for picture making, and so little has been used before, it has a fine freshness for audiences." The lure of the dunes, as a convenient, picturesque site for lost covered wagons, where a generator-powered wind machine could whip up an instant world-class sandstorm, proved as irresistible to John Sturges as it had to John Ford. Within hours after Ford's company shifted their resources to the southern reaches of the monument, the *Walking Hills* crew was earnestly burying their pioneer Conestoga wagon props under small mountains of sand, a couple of miles east of Stovepipe Wells.

The principal players in *The Walking Hills* were Randolph Scott and Ella Raines, supported by William Kennedy, John Ireland, and character actor Edgar Buchanan. Scott, a versatile actor who had starred in musicals, comedies, and World War II adventures, was ultimately renowned as a cowboy hero, naturally gravitating toward the Hollywood westerns that suited his lanky, laconic bearing. Another cast member of note was Josh White, an African-American balladeer, influential guitar stylist, civil rights activist, actor, and former confidant of President Franklin D. Roosevelt.

Assigned once again by T. R. Goodwin to keep an eagle eye by day on the activities of a film crew in the sand dunes, at night Stan Jones morphed into

a singing ranger, strapping on his four-string Martin and treating the cast and crew to his growing repertoire of original songs. The story, repeated endlessly, of how Stan was "discovered" in Death Valley while singing around a campfire to a group of movie location scouts, has only a sketchy modicum of truth to it. In the nine days that *The Walking Hills* company was ensconced at Stovepipe, Stan had an enthusiastic, captive audience to entertain. Chief among his many new fans was leading man Randolph Scott. It was Scott more than anyone else who was convinced that "Ghost Riders in the Sky" could become a hit song, and it was at his urging, rooted in his confidence in Stan's talent after watching him perform night after night, that gave Stan the gumption he needed to head to Los Angeles and try to get his songs published.

That same spring, Stan rode herd over one last band of cinematic bank robbers on the run, desperately plowing through the sand dunes in a frantic search for water. On May 26, another film company arrived to take over Furnace Creek Ranch, this one from Twentieth Century Fox studios to shoot scenes for *Yellow Sky*, a movie directed by William A. Wellman. Starring Gregory Peck, Anne Baxter, and Richard Widmark, the story that ensues from this bank stealing leads the band of desperados, after the requisite thirsty slog through Death Valley, to an abandoned town inhabited only by an old gold miner and his feisty tomboyish granddaughter. The outlaws are torn between stealing the old man's gold stash and Gregory Peck's sudden

The tenor guitar Stan used to compose "Ghost Riders" and a number of other songs. He scratched the names and dates of his inspirations onto the guitar's surface. *Courtesy of Keeter Stuart*

shift in morality inspired by his flourishing respect and fondness for the granddaughter, played by Baxter. Stan didn't get a chance to display his creative talents for this crew, but he and Gregory Peck had taken a shine to each other on the set and ended up as life-long friends.

In order to "remain in the valley to keep in close touch with the motion picture companies," Goodwin had opted to postpone his move up to summer headquarters in Wildrose, though the rest of his staff did so in late May. He reported: "The sets were always left in good condition with little disturbance noted. All movie companies cooperated and it was a pleasure to work with such a fine group of men." The film companies obviously shared Superintendent Goodwin's glow of good cheer. In a rare display of formal appreciation by a major movie studio, the end credits of Twentieth Century Fox's *Yellow Sky* feature a single frame that reads:

> Acknowledgment is gratefully made to the United States Department of Interior for the assistance of its National Park Service, which made possible the filming of this picture in Death Valley National Monument.

For his part, Ranger Stanley D. Jones had a slew of good reasons to be grateful that Hollywood had found a temporary home in Death Valley during that fateful spring. Stan had composed and begun performing "Ghost Riders" sometime in 1947. When he carved "Riders in the Sky 6/5/48" onto the face of his guitar after his meteoric rise to fame and fortune a year later, Stan had saluted a symbolic beginning in his life, not the day he wrote his famous song. New Year's Day of 1944 marked a genesis of adult responsibility for Stan with his marriage to Olive. Four years later, on June 5, 1948, his thirty-fourth birthday, he had set his resolve to follow Randolph Scott's advice: he was determined to find a way to publish his songs.

CHAPTER 8

NATURE BOY

AFTER THE MOVIE COMPANIES HAD PACKED UP AND MOVED ON, THE torrid summer heat settled inexorably into the valley. Stan kept up his routine daily patrols, keeping an eye peeled for unlucky travelers stranded in the dangerously high temperatures with boiling radiators or vapor-locked engines. He checked that the emergency roadside radiator water barrels were full and leak-free, continued to take the daily weather observations at Cow Creek, and hauled the mail from the Furnace Creek Post Office up to Wildrose summer headquarters. Stan was now committed to his new personal mission as well: to act on Randolph Scott's testimony that his songs were worthy of being heard beyond the remote reaches of Death Valley. Olive gave her unwavering support, wholeheartedly urging Stan to plan a sojourn to Los Angeles to shop his songs to music publishing houses.

Stan journeyed to Cow Creek and asked Chief Ranger Ted Ogston's wife, Helen, to notate a song for him. A teacher at the Death Valley elementary school, she was also a classically trained musician and an accomplished pianist. At Helen's behest, Stan strapped on his guitar, put one boot up on her piano stool, and sang the composition that had become the sure-fire favorite of his Death Valley audiences. Helen Ogston recalled her reaction: "Gee Stan, that's a good piece of work, that's a fine song." She went on to say, "He called it 'Ghost Riders in the Sky' and I notated the song for the first time. I later wrote a piano accompaniment for the song and I took that down to Stovepipe Wells—Stanley was going to Hollywood and he went over and picked up the music that I had written and took it with him." By then, Stan had bought a used car and was granted two weeks annual leave for the end of August and the beginning of September. With his cherished wife Olive, his guitar, and Helen Ogston's transcription of "Ghost Riders," Stan headed down the highway to Hollywood, where an implausible, unimaginable future loomed on the horizon.

It was not an auspicious start for the eager songwriter from the wilds of the Death Valley desert, but he was able to get his boots into a few doors. Randolph Scott had hooked Stan up with the band the Sons of the Pioneers, the premier purveyors of smooth, harmonized western tunes. While expressing interest in a few of Stan's songs, including "Beyond The Purple Hills" and "No One Here But Me," they passed on "Ghost Riders" for being dirge-like and "too wordy." (Years later, lead singer Bob Nolan admitted that it was one of the worst decisions he'd ever made in his life.) Stan had also received an offer from the American Music Company for songs called "You And Me and The Ol' Houn' Dog" and a Christmas song, "Snowbells And Echoes," that were scheduled to be recorded and released by December of 1949. A group called The Plainsmen had tentatively agreed to record another of Stan's songs, "A Red Rose In The Garden," for Capitol Records.

After this run of encouraging yet marginal nibbles, Stan, knowing in his heart that "Ghost Riders" was the key to a breakthrough, switched strategies and decided to record a demo of the song to shop around. In those days, the larger music stores had cubicle-style recording booths that housed a *Presto* direct-to-disc recorder, enabling anyone to walk in off the street with a guitar and cut a 78-rpm acetate disc. Stan had just finished recording "Ghost Riders in the Sky" when he crossed paths with Eden Ahbez at the music store.

A diminutive, long-haired, and bearded man bearing a resemblance to a generic image of Jesus, Ahbez insisted that only the words God, Nature, Love, and Happiness deserved to be capitalized and therefore preferred to be known simply as "ahbe." He was a free spirit who roamed the Southern California streets in flowing robes and sandals; subsisted solely on fruits, nuts, and vegetables; and often camped with his wife Anna on the mountain slopes overlooking Tinseltown near the Hollywood sign. He also happened to be the composer of "Nature Boy," the song that Ward Bond had sung incessantly in Death Valley during the filming of *3 Godfathers*. Despite his

Eden Ahbez. *Photo courtesy of Joe Romersa, Shadow Box Studio*

unorthodox appearance, he had cachet in the Hollywood music community, earned after "Nature Boy" became a huge number one hit for Nat King Cole.

The story of how a serene pioneer hippie brought his song to Nat Cole reads like a classic Hollywood fairy tale. In an extraordinary 1948 interview in New York City on the very first televised installment of the long-standing radio show *We The People*, Ahbez, as he was being introduced by the program's host, strode purposefully onstage into the camera's view, pushing his bicycle. He carefully set the bike down and then dropped to the floor where he calmly sat cross-legged on the stage with his prepared script in hand. The host squatted down with his microphone and asked, "Ahbe? How did you happen to write 'Nature Boy'?" Eden, reading somewhat mechanically from the script, answered, "'Nature Boy' is really the story of my life. I was born with a love for nature and a desire to find God. Finally I came to look upon nature as a great symphony and upon love as the theme of that great symphony and suddenly one day a melody just started singing inside of me. So I came down from the hills and went to the theater."

The theater was the Lincoln Theater in Los Angeles, where Nat King Cole was in concert with his trio. After being denied access backstage, Ahbez had pressed a worn envelope that contained the words and music to "Nature Boy" into the theater doorman's hand.[1] The envelope found its way to Cole, who, intrigued by the deceptively simple melody and lyrics, soon began performing the song to the delight of his audiences. In order to release a recording of "Nature Boy," the songwriter had to be credited for the publishing rights, but Eden had neglected to leave his contact information in the envelope.

It was at this point in the *We The People* interview that Nat King Cole glided onstage to meet Eden Ahbez for the first time. Eden stood up from the floor to shake hands with the man who had "played such an important part in [his] life." Cole, with an amused gleam in his eye, continued the story: "Well, I started a search for this strange fellow who left this song with me and I had to leave on a road tour before I found him." Eden chimed in on cue to describe the happy ending, "Yes, and while Nat was traveling, his friend found me."

Eden—who was camped out in Central Park, calling it "the best hotel in the city"—responded to the host's query as to what he was planning to do with the money he had made on "Nature Boy." "All the money in the world will not change my way of life," he said, "because all the money in the world could not give me the things that I already have. Anna and I have learned that a simple life will bring you peace and happiness. We sleep on the ground in sleeping bags in the California mountains and deserts." He did finally allow he was going to buy a jeep to "get me back to nature faster." Then it was Cole's turn to announce: "Well, before you head back to the desert again Eden, we the Nat King Cole Trio would like to play our arrangement of 'Nature Boy.'" Cole moved over to his piano bench and the Trio proceeded to serenade the simulcast radio and television audience with the enchanting song that had sprung from the mystic depths of the "strange fellow" with the beatific smile, who resumed sitting cross-legged on the floor of the stage.

Call it God's will, providence, kismet, destiny, or simply a stroke of ser-

---

[1] Ahbez reportedly kept his verbal agreement with the doorman to share 30 percent of any royalties that he received if the song were ever published.

endipity. Regardless of what cosmic forces conspired to put Stan Jones, in cowboy boots, fringed leather jacket, and Stetson hat, face-to-face with the diminutive Biblical-looking character, Eden Ahbez, in a Hollywood music store, this was Stan's proverbial lucky break. The two men, with equally fantastical addresses, Death Valley and the hills of Hollywood, shared an emphatic love for the natural world, and both had an innate ability to express themselves creatively through songwriting. Ahbez, impressed by the power and sincerity of Stan's songs and the fact that he lived deep in the California desert, asked for a copy of the record of "Ghost Riders" that Stan had just produced, telling him that he knew someone who might be interested in hearing it. Having no reason to believe that this exchange would amount to much, the Joneses returned to Death Valley so that Stan could get back to his Park Service job. Meanwhile, Eden Ahbez had contacted his friend Burl Ives, telling him, "I have a song I think you'll like."

The Joneses returned to Death Valley from Hollywood in early September 1948 and soon settled back into their quiet routine at Emigrant. Stan and all NPS hands were on deck to help move Wildrose summer headquarters back to Cow Creek and reopen the Furnace Creek campgrounds, while the Borax Company readied their hotel facilities at the Inn and Ranch in preparation for the monument's upcoming winter tourist season.

While chatting with his local buddies, Stan expressed hope that a few of his songs that had been received warmly in Hollywood just might make the grade. T. R. Goodwin was not a member of that circle, but rumors of Stan's efforts on the songwriting front reached Cow Creek. Goodwin's garbled mention of Stan's songwriting efforts for the Superintendent's Report for November reads: "Ranger Stanley Jones has submitted three songs, quite appropriate to the times 'Sky Writers in the Sky' [sic] to Bing Crosby and The Mills Brothers publishing house and have been accepted for release in January 1949."

Headlines in the February 4, 1949, edition of the local Inyo County paper, the *Inyo Independent*, crowed "Death Valley Park Ranger Hits Song Jackpot; Numerous Numbers Hailed." The article, bearing the clear imprint of Stan's biggest cheerleader in the valley, George Palmer Putnam, runs down the list of songs lumped in with "Ghost Riders" that were "scheduled" to be recorded and released. Putnam, who is mentioned in the story as being "experienced in musical and motion picture matters," boasted that Stan's Christmas song "Snowbells and Echoes" "has the same lilt that made 'Jingle Bells' immortal, and the universal appeal of 'White Christmas' as well. It's my guess we'll be hearing from Ranger Jones in a big way." The major's prediction would eventually prove to be prescient, but with no help from the songs "No One Here But Me," "A Red Rose in the Garden," "Snowbells and Echoes," and "You and Me and the Ol' Houn' Dog."

By February a few other media dispatches had leaked into Cow Creek, prompting T. R. Goodwin to note: "Ranger Jones continues to gain in prominence from his copyrighted songs of the West." Then, with a glimmer of wishful thinking, he added, "It won't be long until Stan will be using his time exclusively for his new talents and we wish him great success." Stan remained upbeat about his prospects, yet remained almost hopelessly out of touch with events in Hollywood. Word from the outside world traveled slowly to the Emigrant Ranger Station.

Stan journeyed to San Francisco with a team of rangers in February to take part in "Death Valley Week." Jim and Rita Donnelly, who owned a local nursery called the Cacti Garden, organized the gathering held at the Emporium on Market Street. Presentations of slides and talks about Death Valley and other western national parks were scheduled throughout the week. Olive had accompanied her husband on the trip and it was no surprise, given Stan and Olive's outgoing warmth, that they became friends of the Donnellys during their stay. After about a month, the Joneses received a letter back in Death Valley from their new friends, who reported that they had seen an interview in the *San Francisco Chronicle* with Burl Ives. Ives had recently recorded "Riders in the Sky," a tune that was beginning to garner attention in the press, and he confessed that the "forest ranger" in Death Valley who wrote "Riders" was a bit of a mystery to him. This was one of the first inklings for the Joneses that something was afoot.

April of 1949 turned out to be the "greatest visitor month in the history of the Monument" and Easter Sunday, April 9, the single busiest day. Stan and a handful of rangers once again helped Major Putnam set the large white cross in place for the traditional Easter Sunrise Service held annually in the sand dunes. The "entire force" was employed to prepare for the service by hauling a piano from Furnace Creek Ranch to the dunes, constructing a platform for the choir, and installing a public address system. T. R. Goodwin's glowing review of the service read:

> The rather hurriedly prepared Easter Sunrise Service was very well attended
> and a complete success. The chorus of twenty voices, all local people from
> Beatty, Death Valley Junction and employees of the National Park Service
> and Death Valley Hotel Company had been organized, trained, and con-
> ducted by Mrs. Helen Ogston and gave an almost professional performance
> accompanied on the Solo Vox by Mrs. Floyd Keller. Both these Park Service
> wives worked extremely hard to whip together this untrained chorus and
> the results were distinctly satisfactory and enjoyed by the large audience.

Despite the bustling holiday crowds on the monument's roadways during
the week, all park rangers ably assisted in presenting evening programs in the
hotel lobbies and around fire circles in the campgrounds, reaching out to a
total of more than five thousand visitors. John Nugie, at that time a college
student from California, fondly recalled his time spent with Ranger Jones:

> In April, 1949, I was in Death Valley with a group from University of the
> Pacific on the school's annual trip to Death Valley to study geology, plant,
> and animal life. We camped out at Stovepipe Wells and at our evening
> campfire a young park ranger named Stan Jones joined us with his guitar
> and led the singing. The last song he sang he introduced as one he had
> written and hoped to have recorded. The song was "Ghost Riders in the
> Sky." We loved it so much that he sang it over and over before we would
> let him go. In fact I and another friend invited him to go with our group
> the following day to lecture about the desert plants, which he did. What a
> great experience that I will never forget.

After the heavy Easter travel period ended, Stan and his fellow rangers went to
work rehabbing all the improvised roadside campsites that had sprung up due
to the huge swarm of visitors. Superintendent Goodwin reported a number
of other employee activities for the month, recording that "several new signs
were posted, others touched up that were damaged" and that "nine burros
were disposed of in the Wildrose area." These were Stan's final halcyon days as
a National Park Service ranger. The song he had written one Sunday morning
at the Emigrant Ranger Station was about to alter his life forever.

CHAPTER 9

ALL THE STARS
OF DEATH VALLEY

WHEN EDEN AHBEZ GAVE THE DEMO PRESSING OF "GHOST RIDERS IN the Sky" to Burl Ives, he unleashed a chain of events destined to transform Stan and Olive's lives. Ives, enjoying a multi-faceted career in Hollywood after being cast as a singing cowboy for the film *Smoky* in 1945, originally hailed from Indiana. Blessed with a smooth, golden husk of a voice, Ives had wandered the United States during the Depression years as an itinerant folk singer, finally landing in New York in 1940. There he acquired his own CBS radio show, named after one of the many traditional American ballads that he had popularized, "The Wayfaring Stranger." He fell in with the loose aggregation of the Almanac Singers, who included at various turns Woody Guthrie, Will Geer, Pete Seeger, Leadbelly, and Josh White, who combined to perform concerts benefiting civil rights causes in New York City and up and down the eastern seaboard. Drafted into the Army in 1942 but medically discharged the following year, Ives wound up in Hollywood and slowly began to build a rewarding career as a versatile film actor and Columbia Records recording artist.

Burl Ives and Eden Ahbez arranged to meet at the Brown Derby on Vine Street in Hollywood, where Ahbez gave Ives the record of Stan singing "Ghost Riders." Ives later recalled, "I went home, played it, and thought it was wonderful." He promptly recognized the song's potential and arranged with Columbia Records to record "Ghost Riders" in mid-February of 1949, deciding to adopt Stan's unadorned arrangement from the demo of lone voice and guitar. *Billboard*, the weekly trade magazine for all phases of the entertainment industry, picked up the story. Dated "Hollywood, February 26," under the heading of "Ain't Nature Boy Grand; Eden Spurs Riders in the Sky," *Billboard* reported:

> Eden (Nature Boy) Ahbez, relatively quiet since his tune scored a smash last year, cropped up in the music trade again this week. This time he made news in the role of godfather to a neophyte cleffer[1] by lending a hand to Stan Jones, a Death Valley forest ranger and part-time songwriter.
>
> Thru Ahbez's aid Jones was able to present his new folk ditty *Riders in the Sky* to balladeer Burl Ives. After fast consultation Ives immediately waxed the tune for Columbia. Pubber Buddy Morris got wind of the pitch and bought the publishing rights after outbidding rivals.
>
> Jones's song, based on an old western legend, created a terrific stir in the local music fraternity. Columbia is rushing record release date to give the platter top priority, while Morris will have sheet music out in several weeks.

In a highly unusual foreword, printed on the sheet music for "Riders," Burl Ives, pictured grim-faced and wearing a black cowboy hat above the text, described the appeal that Stan's song held:

> I have always believed that folk music is a living, growing thing, not entirely traditional with roots only in the past. "Riders in the Sky,"[2] the first published song of a young forest ranger named Stan Jones seems, to me at any rate, to bear out my belief.
>
> Here is a contemporary, composed ballad, with all the elements of true folk music. It tells a story. It has rich imagery in its language, and it has music of imagination and integrity.
>
> It was from this record that Stan Jones sold "Riders in the Sky" to his publishers, and I wish him and them much success with it. I know they will have it.

The Burl Ives rendition of Ranger Jones's song, although unique for its spare production value, failed to make an immediate splash on the *Billboard* charts. But Stan's song began to make the rounds between music industry

---

[1] *Billboard* articles from the era are filled with music industry shorthands: a "cleffer" is a songwriter, a "pubber" the publisher of the song, and "waxed" translates as recorded.
[2] Stan's song was published by Edwin H. Morris and Company, Inc. as "Riders in the Sky (A Cowboy Legend)."

The original published sheet music of "Riders In The Sky: A Cowboy Legend"
Courtesy of Michael Ward

insiders and found its way to the right guy. Bandleader and vocalist Vaughn Monroe had been on the lookout for another cowboy-style tune to follow up on the surprise success of his initial foray into the western music genre, a

1948 version of "Blue Shadows On The Trail." Leading a versatile orchestra that had enjoyed a string of number-one hits for RCA Records since the early 1940s, Monroe hit pay dirt when he got a call from Charles Grean. Grean, who worked with both pop and country artists, sat on a panel of RCA employees who regularly listened to demo recordings in hopes of finding new "hits" for the label. Grean practically jumped out of his chair when he first heard the demo of "Riders in the Sky." This is how he remembered hearing Stan's song for the first time:

> As soon as I heard it, I said "Oh my God! What a piece of material. What an idea! Let me have this song. I'll get Vaughn Monroe to do it!" I called Monroe up, and found out he was going to be in Milwaukee, and he would have an open date in Chicago in a few days. I said, "All right we're going to book you into the Chicago studio. I'll come out and bring you the song. You can learn it overnight."

Recorded in Chicago on March 14, 1949, Monroe's stellar arrangement of eerily muted brass figures and the haunting "yipi-yi-ay, yipi-yi-o" background vocals that wrapped around his rich baritone voice, ran roughshod over the earnest, folk-oriented version by Burl Ives. Vaughn Monroe's recording of "Riders in the Sky (A Cowboy Legend)" took the American airwaves by storm and immediately sent shivers down the collective spines of radio listeners throughout the land. Monroe's version of Stan's song first appeared on the *Billboard* charts on April 15, where it remained for twenty-two weeks, peaking at number one. "Riders in the Sky" proceeded to smash all previous sales figures in the history of RCA Victor Records, quickly surpassing the mark set the previous year by Spike Jones with his novelty song, "Two Front Teeth."

An article in *Billboard* emanating from New York City dated April 23 read:

> Vaughn Monroe's "Riders in the Sky" is selling at a record-breaking pace, according to a Victor sales report, having gone over 300,000 in its first two weeks. Under the hit-it-while-it's-hot approach, the waxery is going all-out promotion-wise, and will have a dirigible over the city Saturday, flashing the platter title and playing the record over a p.a. system. The Detroit distributor for RCA is planning a stunt in which *luminous cutouts of steers will be hauled over the city by airplane.*

Bing Crosby jumped on the "Cowboy Legend" bandwagon and recorded "Riders in the Sky," modeled after Burl Ives's version, on March 22. It entered the charts on May 6 and lasted for six weeks, topping out at position fourteen. A snappy rendition by Peggy Lee was recorded on April 18 and enjoyed reasonable success on the *Billboard* charts, while Bob Nolan and his Sons of the Pioneers swallowed a little crow and soon recorded their fine arrangement of the song deemed "too wordy" by Nolan only a few months earlier. Burl Ives's recording was carried along by the incredible wave of popularity of "Riders" and his original version finally hit the Billboard charts on April 22 and stayed there for six weeks. By June of 1949, there were no less than thirteen separate recordings of "Riders in the Sky" by renowned American artists of the era simultaneously available in record stores. Pedro Vargas, "The Nightingale of the Americas," recorded "Jinetes En El Cielo" (Riders in the Sky), a rendition faithful to Vaughn Monroe's, and his version of Stan's song became a giant hit in Mexico.

The song had become so huge and so ubiquitous that musical prankster Spike Jones, perhaps suffering from a bout of sour grapes over the sales of Stan's song rapidly eclipsing "Two Front Teeth," couldn't resist jumping into the mix by recording a parody of Monroe's version. At the end of May, RCA Victor Records released Spike's satiric take of "Riders in the Sky," featuring a couple of grossly inebriated cowpokes struggling haplessly to join in on the "yipi-yi-ay, yipi-yi-o" chorus. Inspired by a *Time* magazine article that compared the opening notes of Stan's song to "the first few steps of 'When Johnny Comes Marching Home,'" Jones ended his spoof with: "When Johnny comes marching home again, hooray, hooray / We make the guy who wrote this song pay and pay / 'Cause all we hear is 'Ghost Riders' sung by Vaughn Monroe / I can do without his singing, but I wish I had his dough." Monroe was not amused and wielded his influence as a major shareholder in RCA Victor to have Jones's record pulled off the shelves, making copies of the original release a valuable collector's item to this day.

Back at his post in Death Valley, Stan became agreeably aware of the runaway popularity of "Ghost Riders" in the guise of a substantial royalty check from his publisher, Buddy Morris. He immediately journeyed to Los Angeles to collect the cash and bought a brand new Oldsmobile 88. The success of his song, dreamed up on the front porch of the Emigrant Ranger Station, continued to build. A scant three weeks had passed since the song first appeared on the radio. In the superintendent's report for April, T. R. Goodwin summed up the whirlwind of publicity that had suddenly enveloped Death Valley's Singing Ranger:

Caught between two worlds: Stan's new 1949 Rocket 88 Oldsmobile bought with his first royalty check, parked outside Emigrant Station. His NPS patrol vehicle sits at the entrance to the Jones's living quarters. *Allan Grant / The LIFE Picture Collection / Getty Images*

> The tremendous success as a songwriter . . . has come so rapidly to Ranger Stanley Jones that it seems almost incredible to Jones himself as well as to his associates. His western songs with which he frequently entertained friends and visitors were taken more or less as a matter of course until heard by Randolph Scott and Ella Raines while making a picture here a year ago. Invited to Hollywood he became an overnight sensation, his song "Riders in the Sky" being sung by Burl Ives, Bing Crosby and Vaughn Monroe and on the radio on most of the hit song reviews. *Newsweek* and *Time* wrote him up and *Life* sent photographers for an illustrated article. His Victor record has already sold over 300,000 copies and he has motion picture and radio contracts and a European tour in prospect.

Superintendent Goodwin wrapped up his review of Stan's new fortunes somewhat peevishly: "It does not seem possible that he can do justice to his ranger position much longer and give so much of his time to this outside interest."

The writer and photographer sent by *Life* to Emigrant in late April were clearly on a mission to produce a major article on Stan, summarizing his work as a Death Valley ranger, to tell the story of the "discovery" of "Ghost Riders," and to showcase his life in the desert with Olive. Over a hundred photographs of Ranger Jones in action during the course of his routine NPS duties were snapped: obviously staged shots of Stan (who had arrived on the scene in his new Oldsmobile) helping a motorist change a tire, putting the gear together that he routinely carried in his NPS pickup, poring over a map before heading out on patrol, checking the radiator water barrels along the roads, and recording the daily weather.

A series of photos of Stan moonlighting as the Singing Ranger featured him strumming his guitar to a number of staged "cowpokes" slouched around a blazing campfire with the obligatory pot of cowboy coffee set nearby. The shots of his leisure activities with Olive featured the couple picnicking at the sand dunes, preparing for a horseback ride at Furnace Creek, and Stan entertaining a crowd at the Stovepipe Wells lounge as Olive radiantly smiles from a barstool. Another series of photos shows the Joneses relaxing at home with Olive typing in the background while Stan, posed with guitar and pencil in hand over a sheet of music, appears to be on the verge of churning out another blockbuster song.

The *Life* team, against Olive's forceful protests, insisted on adding a beer and a cigarette to Stan's songwriting tableau at the ranger station's living quarters, promising over and over again that those photos would not be used for the upcoming article. In the June 27, 1949, issue, the resulting "article" didn't mention Death Valley at all and consisted solely of a single 3½ x 2½ inch black and white photo above the heading "Stan Jones" with a meager two-sentence blurb underneath: "The former Arizona cowhand, who composed songs for dude vacationers, suddenly became famous when one of them, *Riders in the Sky*, hit the top in sheet-music sales, records, the Hit Parade. With his royalties he plans to buy a ranch." In a typical display of media arrogance, the photograph chosen features Stan with a Camel dangling from his mouth and a bottle of Lucky Lager set prominently on the table in the foreground. Olive, during an interview nearly sixty years later, still seethed that the *Life* reporters had broken their vow: her Mormon folk in Idaho were not smokers or drinkers.

The May 2 issue of *Time* had shown up at Cow Creek headquarters with an article heralding Stan as the "leathery-necked U.S. forest ranger" who had written the wildly popular new song, "Riders in the Sky." Entitled "Roweling Hard" (a rowel is the spiked, revolving disc at the end of a spur), the article featured a quote from Stan that was often repeated in subsequent media stories: "Most rangers marry schoolteachers, doggoned if I know why." Whether or not he actually said this is open to question. A number of other cavalier quotes and downright fictitious tales flooded the print media regarding the

Stan Jones "composing" a new song with Olive in the background. Despite Olive's fervent protests, this was the only photograph published in the June 27, 1949, issue of *Life* magazine. *Allan Grant / The LIFE Picture Collection / Getty Images*

Singing Ranger's biography, with many of the juiciest whoppers emanating from Stan himself. The *Time* article, one of the more factual renderings of how "Ghost Riders" came into the public eye, credited Randolph Scott and Eden Ahbez as the main players helping the song to see the light of day. The editors, perhaps to keep pace with other more flamboyant portrayals of the song, decided to spice up the prose by adding that "Riders" "had hair on its chest, and would be hard to croon with mush in the mouth" and that "Riders was roweling hard for the top of the *Hit Parade*."

Newsweek, in its May 2 edition, was a tad dismissive of Stan's song in a piece called "Riding High" and reads as a rather snobbish backlash against the colossal popularity of "Ghost Riders." Perhaps attempting to distinguish itself from its counterpart and major competitor, *Time, Newsweek* accused "Riders" of being "reminiscent of any number of folk tunes," a "pseudo-cowboy song," and "a natural for exploitation." The article derides Vaughn Monroe's version as "all dressed up, with muted trumpets and a chorus singing through an echo chamber," while touting Burl Ives's arrangement as "simpler and more in keeping with the folk spirit of the song." Stan is portrayed as a "forest ranger" and an "itinerant performer around Death Valley," who had written a few songs before that "never amounted to much."

Even with all the attention from the media, Stan expressed his discouragement to Olive that he hadn't yet heard "Riders in the Sky" where it mattered the most in 1949. The gold standard for the true measure of a song in that era wasn't its position on the *Billboard* charts, but whether or not it appeared on the Saturday night radio show, *Your Hit Parade*. An advertising agency produced the immensely popular show, which chose the nation's top ten hit songs each week based on consultation with music shops about sheet music sales and by interviewing band leaders to compile their most requested songs.

Media communications in 1949 were far from instantaneous and the results often took weeks to tabulate, creating a lag between when a song was posted on the charts and when it actually achieved a hallowed spot on *Your Hit Parade*. The broadcast featured an in-house studio orchestra playing charts that faithfully replicated the original recordings of the featured songs of the week. Punctuated by commercials for Lucky Strike cigarettes featuring tobacco auctioneers, the week's top ten songs were sung in descending order by a renowned singer of the day. Even though Vaughn Monroe's version of "Riders in the Sky" played all over the American airwaves, Stan, usually confined to the desert wilderness of Death Valley, had still not heard his song on *Your Hit Parade*. April passed, and on into May, Stan and Olive, with fingers crossed, kept tuning into *Your Hit Parade* on the radio in the Oldsmobile 88 on Saturday nights at Emigrant. "Riders" had not appeared in any of the top ten songs yet and they grew more disappointed as the weeks wore on.

Saturday, May 21, 1949, was not a particularly momentous day in the history of the United States. Eleanor Roosevelt, in her daily letter to the American people, expressed shock at her discovery that the state of Vermont could still throw people who were behind on their bills into debtor's prison. Jackie

Stan and Olive Jones in Death Valley, 1949. *Allan Grant / The LIFE Picture Collection / Getty Images*

Robinson earned six RBIs as the visiting Brooklyn Dodgers pounded the St. Louis Cardinals, 15–6. An unidentified flying object, described by personnel at a Washington radar station as a "silvery, disc-shaped object," was sighted hovering over the Hanford Atomic Plant at an altitude of approximately 20,000 feet. More locally, on that day in Death Valley a light dusting of snow remained scattered across the high peaks of the Panamints from a late spring storm, and the oncoming evening at Emigrant Ranger Station promised to be mild, clear, and starry. Friends Bob and Mary Foreman, who worked a silver mine twenty miles away in Panamint Valley, had driven east up and over Townes Pass to join the Joneses for what Stan prayed would finally be a celebratory Saturday night.

Stan switched the radio on and the *Hit Parade* countdown began. He grew increasingly dejected as Frank Sinatra and the studio orchestra ran through that week's top ten hits that included "Red Roses For A Blue Lady," "Some Enchanted Evening," and "Cruising Down The River." When Sinatra had finished crooning the number two song of that week's *Hit Parade*, the gentle ballad "Again," Stan resisted the temptation to switch the radio off. Stan, Olive, and the Foremans gamely listened to another Lucky Strike commercial, and then with trumpets blaring and drums rolling, the studio announcer dramatically intoned: "Number one! The top ten tune of the week, the song the survey finds in first place!" The trumpets abruptly halted, the drum roll ceased, and in sudden silence, Frank Sinatra took over: "And tonight we salute a new topper, this song's really ridin' tall in the saddle: 'Ghost Riders in the Sky'!" And there it was: the rolling guitar introduction, the muted brass figure echoing the riders' "yipi-yi-ay, yipi-yi-o" call of the background vocals, and the singular voice of Frank Sinatra, tearing into Stan's song like it was his very own. In a 2006 interview, Olive, mist in her eyes as she finished recounting this moment that she had shared with her husband, simply said, "All the stars of Death Valley came falling from the sky."

CHAPTER 10

WE HOPE HE MAKES A MILLION DOLLARS

STAN, FINALLY BLESSED WITH THE VALIDATION HE HAD YEARNED FOR, braced himself as the floodgates of demand opened wide for personal appearances by "Stan Jones, the Singing Ranger." Superintendent Goodwin appeared of two minds in his May memorandum to the Regional Director. Under the heading of General Publicity, Goodwin wrote: "With the great success story being written around the 'Death Valley Ranger' Stanley Jones much publicity has been received of course for Death Valley." On the other hand he had a monument to run and under the heading of Protection he groused: "The continued absence of Ranger Stanley Jones from his station at Emigrant Junction except for a day or two weekly made it imperative to correct the neglect at this key entrance station and it was decided to assign Ranger Houston to that station and move Jones to Wildrose until such time as he decided whether or not to leave the Service to attend to his increasingly personal business."

The Singing Ranger's "increasingly personal business" included agreeing to a term contract "following several weeks of negotiation," to be represented by William Morris, America's premier talent agency. *Billboard* magazine reported:

> [William Morris] will give Jones fast build-up to cash in his whirlwind
> prominence and is planning a personal appearance tour, disk contract and
> possible picture deals. Jones, who so far continues to hold down a regular

Stan's Mercury Records version of "Riders In The Sky," recorded in May, 1949. *Courtesy of Keeter Stuart*

job as a national park ranger in Death Valley, is expected to ink the record pact next week with a major record company, to be featured as a warbler and instrumentalist.

By the end of May, Stan had recorded his version of "Ghost Riders" on the Mercury label, billed as Stan Jones and His Death Valley Rangers. A brief review in *Billboard* of Stan's effort was upbeat yet realistic:

> Jones, the composer of the meteoric range song, sings a fervent rendition of his tune, with steady-beat guitar, echoed vocal group in back, etc. Will get plenty play, but won't press earlier versions.

The earlier versions of "Riders in the Sky" referred to could have only meant Vaughn Monroe's. His RCA recording still rode atop the nation's popular music charts and the sales figures continued to skyrocket. Stan was flabbergasted by the amount of the first big payoff from his publishing company. On one trip to Hollywood, Ranger Jones sought out his kindred spirit and fellow songwriter Eden Ahbez. In an incredibly magnanimous gesture, Stan offered Ahbez $50,000 for his pivotal role in helping to popularize "Ghost Riders," exactly half the sum of Stan's first royalty check. Even though Ahbez's largess from the sales of "Nature Boy" was tied up by a lawsuit[1] at the time, he was blissfully content with his accustomed three-dollar-a-week subsistence mode while living under the stars, and politely turned down Stan's offer.

Superintendent Goodwin, in order to assuage the demands of the mounting mobs of curious visitors showing up at headquarters clamoring to meet the now famous Park Service ranger, asked Stan and Olive to move to Cow Creek. Stan's response was a swift, "Ollie, we've gotta get outta here!" It wasn't so cut and dried though, for Stan now had a real dilemma facing him. He was basically a blue-collar guy who loved his job as a Death Valley ranger, and, despite the rampant success of "Ghost Riders," there were no guarantees that his musical talents would carry him and Olive forward finan-cially. Stan had suffered through too many lean years to just walk away from a regular paycheck and a permanent government job with all the attendant benefits. He decided to approach Goodwin and ask for a year's leave of ab-sence. The Superintendent, still not particularly keen on his ranger's refusal to shoot burros, wasn't interested in accommodating Stan's request: It was flatly denied.

During his final weeks with the National Park Service, Stan gamely tried to balance his ranger responsibilities with a flurry of promotional appear-ances and business meetings in Hollywood, but it was becoming clear that something had to give. He was driving back and forth to Southern Califor-nia in his Rocket 88, burning up what leave time he had left, in an ultimately futile attempt to straddle his boots across two widely disparate worlds.

With his hand finally forced by the reality of his newfound fame, Stan reluctantly agreed to quit his job as a park ranger for good on June 21. In the Superintendent's report for June of 1949, T. R. Goodwin inserted one last swipe at the Singing Ranger, noting, "Ranger Houston has been moved to Emigrant Station following the departure of Ranger Jones and the seri-ous situation of lack of service and attention at Emigrant Junction has now been remedied." He then obligingly adds, "Ranger Stanley Jones submitted his resignation to give his entire time to his songwriting and record making activities. He was given a farewell party by the entire Monument group on the 21st and departed for New York the following day."

---

[1] A Yiddish composer, Herman Yablokoff, claimed that Ahbez "borrowed" the melody for "Nature Boy" from one of his songs. The suit was eventually settled out of court with a settlement in Yablokoff's favor.

The party was held at a small building used for social events at Wildrose summer headquarters. George Pipkin recalled it as "the chilliest he had ever attended." In an effort to obtain his desired leave of absence, Stan had apparently attempted an end run around the superintendent by making a plea to the Western Regional Director. T. R. Goodwin, whom Olive described as "a funny little man," showed his snippy displeasure by staying out on the front porch, separate from the main party, smoking his pipe, and passing the time chatting with a handful of employees.

Cookies and punch were served as Stan sang a batch of his songs, topped off, of course, with "Ghost Riders in the Sky." Pipkin captured the strained denouement to the evening and Stan's career as an NPS ranger:

> The later it got, the more embarrassing the party became. It seemed that none of the park people wanted to risk the disfavor of the Superintendent by wishing Stan a fond farewell. Finally old Pipkin could stand the suspense no longer and taking the bull by the horns, he made the speech. We told Stan how much we had enjoyed knowing him and his wife Olive, and how happy we were for his success. We wished him the best of luck and hoped he made a million dollars with his song. The party broke up, Stan and Olive driving away to Hollywood in their new Oldsmobile 88. Pipkins drove down canyon to Wildrose Station in their surplus jeep.

The following day Stan hopped on a plane in Los Angeles for an engagement at the Roxy Theater in New York, where, during the previous week, city dwellers had been treated to the sight of an RCA-financed promotional blimp floating over the metropolis lit with the words: "Hear Vaughn Monroe's Riders in the Sky." Stan's song had rapidly melded itself into the nation's cultural vocabulary. A sports writer for the *Los Angeles Times*, describing a lopsided eleven-run first inning led by a Sacramento team over its opponents in a minor league baseball game, wrote, "Those 'Riders in the Sky' didn't have a thing on Sacramento, which was in front of the herd instead of following it." The lead line in a *Times* story about an unusual "sea mirage" that occurred along the Southern California coast read, "'Ghost Riders in the Sky' above the sea puzzled, then thrilled Santa Monica yesterday." A Midwesterner remembers singing Stan's song in his elementary school classroom, substituting the word "heck" for "hell" in the last verse. A pious Detroit disc jockey who had publicly destroyed a Kay Starr record containing the blasphemous line "He beats the hell out of me" gave Stan's song a pass, explaining that "the literal use of the word, as in 'Riders in the Sky,' was not objectionable."

Even livestock couldn't escape the nationwide obsession with "Ghost Riders." A former Park Service employee who had retired from Mount Rainier before Stan arrived at the park had gone to work on a ranch in eastern Washington. He and his wife were given a small house to reside in and a milk cow. He remembers:

> The cow was a wild thing and it was a challenge to milk her. At that time, one of our favorite songs was "Ghost Riders in the Sky." On summer evenings, we'd crank up the Victrola and Vaughn Monroe's rendition. The cow, Josephine, grazed in the pasture right behind the house. When the song played, she would go wild, pacing up and down the fence, rolling her eyes and emitting a low moan. No other song affected her that way, and when the music stopped, she would calm down.

By late June, Burl Ives's version of "Riders" was still among the top ten songs on *Billboard*'s Folk/Country & Western charts. RCA Victor continued its massive promotional push to keep Vaughn Monroe's record at the top of the charts. In Salt Lake City consumers were given a shot at winning $100 and 100 records by providing the best answer to "I like Vaughn Monroe's 'Riders in the Sky' because . . ." An RCA rep in Los Angeles had arranged with Western Airlines to name a plane "The Sky Rider," with customers being able to enjoy the inaugural flight accompanied by the Sons of the Pioneers. A memo to "All RCA Victor Record Distributors" dated June 20, urging employees to find fresh, creative ways to sell more records, ended with: "Flash! Sales nationally as of June 10 were 1,138,034 records." On July 7, 1949, RCA had announced that Vaughn Monroe's disc of "Ghost Riders in the Sky" had sold an unprecedented 1,800,000 copies in the previous two months.

Stan's apprehensions about being able to financially sustain himself and his wife faded into the sunset as the success of "Ghost Riders" carried the Joneses through the remainder of 1949 and beyond. Personal appearances by the songwriting phenom included a stint on the radio drama *This Is Your FBI* as a ranger who helps capture criminals, and an eight-minute song and interview slot on Eddie Cantor's radio show, for which he received the tidy sum of $1,500. Capitalizing on his former profession as a "forest ranger,"[2] Stan, billed as "the Singing Ranger," staged performances wearing his Park Service uniform backed by a male vocal choir dubbed "The Ranger Cho-

---

[2] To this day there is widespread, understandable confusion in the public's mind between the ranger forces of the Department of Agriculture's Forest Service and the Department of Interior's National Park Service. Branded by *Time* magazine as the "leathery-necked forest ranger," Stan was usually aligned by the media with the wrong federal agency thereafter.

rus." The group sang a few of Stan's compositions glorifying the landscapes encompassed by the premier national parks of the west and then broke into versions of his "cowboy" songs, including "Whirlwind," "The Burro Lullaby," "Cowpoke," and "Ghost Riders."

As a solo act on the concert stage, Stan didn't fare so well. He was capable of riveting listeners with his songs around a campfire or in an intimate barroom setting, but tended to fall flat in larger venues. After a performance at the Oriental Theater in Chicago in July 1949, a reviewer wrote:

> Stan Jones, writer of 'Riders in the Sky,' should have stayed at his ranger station in Death Valley and counted his royalties. A pleasant hillbilly yodeler, he fails completely in the stage savvy department. Garbed in cowboy togs, he limped through 'Cattle Call' and followed, after a little talk, with 'Riders.' He has either a weak voice or the p.a. system here should be perked up.

Stan's great friend and fellow musician, Johnny Western, was frank in describing his songwriting mentor's inherent weakness as a performer:

> As much as I loved Stan, he was not a great vocalist. He had his little four-string tenor guitar, sort of like an oversized ukulele—not too much music comes out of it. With that and a combination of Stan's voice, it was like listening to a guy around a campfire that was having fun but who wasn't really a professional. Stan wouldn't have made it as a recording artist, but my God, his writing ability was something I'd never seen before or since.

Lloyd Perryman, a longtime member of the Sons of the Pioneers and a good pal of Stan's, observed:

> It's very unlikely that Stan had much, if any, musical background because of the way he played his little tenor guitar. His lack of being aware whether he put too many beats in a bar or too few beats in a bar would indicate that he had never had any basic musical training. But, boy, the ideas . . . I think the man could have written fifteen songs a day if he'd take a notion, and every one of those songs would have some points of interest that would fascinate anyone who cared about lyrics. He had so many, many beautiful phrases.

Stan simply rode the waves generated by his song and happily obliged the demand for public appearances while the novelty of "Ghost Riders" remained fresh. He even figured a way to get a shot at acting in films. A number of

Gene Autry and Stan Jones re-enacting the deal made for Autry to use the title "Riders In The Sky" for his next feature film. *Everett Collection*

production companies were anxiously aiming to outbid each other for the rights to use "Riders" for a Hollywood western. The William Morris Agency negotiated a package deal with Gene Autry Productions, giving Autry the full-screen rights to use the songs and the titles for future films from two of Stan's compositions, "Riders in the Sky" and "Whirlwind." Per Stan's urging, the agreement included the "acting services of the composer." Autry already had in production a film to be called *Beyond The Purple Hills*. He simply swapped out the name to "Riders in the Sky" and added the expected scenes of ghostly cows being chased by sweaty cowpokes. A new opening scene was filmed that featured Stan loping along next to the cowboy movie star as the opening credits rolled. This was Stan's first time in front of a motion picture camera. The Singing Ranger, riding jauntily along beside Autry, who was lip-synching his own version of "Ghost Riders," is seen in the background occasionally mouthing the chorus of his song with a muffled grin on his face. You can't help but get the sense that he's merrily thinking, "Look Ma, I'm in the movies!"

Stan enjoyed all the attention and novel opportunities thoroughly, but he

Publicity photo of the "Singing Ranger" inscribed by Stan to George and Ann Pipkin. *Courtesy of Margaret Brush*

still harbored a suspicion that this good fortune in the entertainment world wouldn't last. An article in *Parade* magazine featured a photo of Stan and Eden Ahbez perched together atop the jeep that Ahbez had purchased with his initial royalties from "Nature Boy." It stated that Stan intended to stay within his former Park Service salary budget of $3,600 a year. The Singing Ranger then pronounced, "I give myself four more years here in Hollywood and then back to the woods."

The Joneses had rented an apartment on Los Feliz Boulevard that was

Olive Jones at Wildrose Station during a visit with the Pipkins, circa 1953.
Courtesy of Lynn Keller

south of Griffith Park in Los Angeles and just a stone's throw from Holly-wood, but they found themselves on the public relations trail for "Ghost Riders" for much of the summer of 1949. Once the hubbub over Stan's song had finally cooled a bit, Stan and Olive bought a home at Crystal Bay on Lake Tahoe, satisfying their desire to stay in touch with the woods and also to be closer to their respective families in Northern California and South-eastern Idaho. They commuted back and forth as necessary between Los Angeles and Tahoe to meet Stan's continued obligations to his new career.

On stationery with the printed letterhead of "Stan Jones: Songs of the Trail," Olive wrote a note dated September 22, 1949, to her Death Valley friend Ann Pipkin. Olive lamented that she and Stan were unable to accept an invitation to a Saturday evening birthday party for George at Wildrose Station due to Stan being "all tied up the entire weekend." She wrote, hope-fully, "we will see you one of these times on our way through," but by then the consuming reality of Stan's ties to the entertainment industry had indel-ibly changed their lives. Despite his continued lifelong esteem for the National Park Service and the happy memories of his and Olive's shared years at Emigrant, the Joneses rarely returned to Death Valley together.

CHAPTER 11

DON'T WRITE ANYTHING ABOUT CACTUS!

IN THE FALL OF 1949, LUCKY STARS ALIGNED ONCE AGAIN FOR STAN when he was invited to the home of George O'Brien in the Los Angeles suburb of Brentwood. O'Brien had worked with director John Ford back in his silent film days, starring in what is widely acknowledged as Ford's first great film, *Iron Horse*, made in 1924. O'Brien had been estranged from Ford for many years, as was often the case with many of the irascible director's friends and colleagues, but George was now back in good stead with Ford, working again for him in the 1948 film *Fort Apache*. When O'Brien discovered that Stan had been involved with Ford's Death Valley set of *3 Godfathers*, he immediately called his pal, Dobe Carey, gushing, "Drop everything my friend, and get over here. There's a good man here Dobe, who knows you, but you'll never guess who it is until you see him."

Carey drove the short mile over to O'Brien's place and later described his entry into George's living room:

> Rising from the sofa as I entered was none other than the park ranger from
> the deadly sands of Death Valley—the man who had the audacity to tell
> John Ford that you couldn't squeeze water out of a cactus during the film-
> ing of *Three Godfathers*, the year before. It was park ranger Stan Jones.

An animated reunion followed with reminiscences about the Death Valley shoot and talk of Stan's newfound fame as a songwriter. Then O'Brien made the suggestion that John Ford might like to see Stan again, a meeting that Dobe Carey justly claimed "changed many people's lives."

George called Ford asking him if he'd like to hear a song from a "genius of western music," and in a jiffy they were on their way to the RKO Studios in Culver City where Ford sat in his office. Carey remembered, "When we all marched in, Uncle Jack knew Stan right away. He didn't start up about the cactus, like I thought he would, but he never did what you thought he would do. He was really glad to see Stan, and right away, I knew they would get along." The director peppered Stan with questions about his background, how he had begun working for the National Park Service, and about his songwriting. Ford was clearly impressed with this man standing before him, dressed in a fringed suede jacket, Hawaiian shirt, ranger hat, and cowboy boots, with his ever-present guitar slung over his shoulder. Carey, who became a lifelong friend of Ranger Jones, described Stan's curly hair as "spilling out from under his ranger hat in all different directions. It always looked like someone had used an eggbeater on it. He was a pioneer in scooping long hair from one side and plastering it across the bald spot on the top."

Ford called for a song. Stan strapped on his guitar and regaled the group with a stirring version of "Ghost Riders." Seeing that the director was entranced by what he had just heard, Stan ventured, "Mr. Ford, I wrote a sort of sequel to 'Ghost Riders' called 'Rollin' Dust.' I'd like to sing that too, if it's okay. I really like it better, myself." By the end of that song Ford had obviously made up his mind about something. Dobe Carey wrote:

> John Ford took the pipe from his mouth, lifted his feet from off the desk, leaned forward toward Stan, and said, "Great. Great. Just great. But there's one problem." We all looked worried. "I need that song about the ghost town—the one you just sang—for my picture with Ben (Johnson) and Dobe. But I also need two or three more. Can you write three more before I finish the picture? They'll not be sung in the movie, they'll be used in the score after we finish shooting. Is that going to be a problem, Jones?"
>
> Stan exclaimed, "No sir, Mr. Ford. That's not going to be a problem at all. Heck, I can write three songs by tomorrow night. No problem, sir. None at all."

Ford saw to it that Stan, ecstatic with his new songwriting assignment, had a copy of the script in hand for his next western, *Wagon Master*. Scheduled to be filmed in Moab, Utah, *Wagon Master* was the story of a wagon train of

Mormon pioneers who enlist the help of a couple of horse traders, played by Dobe Carey and Ben Johnson, to lead them to a remote valley they have in their sights as "promised land." A run-in with a murderous family of outlaws provides the dramatic force of the story. For guidance as to the nature of the songs he was after, Ford called only for Stan to "follow your own good judgment." He stood up, offered Stan his hand, and then suggested where his judgment might lead him, saying, "You've got a hell of a start with that 'Rollin' Dust' thing. Make the others in the same vein, you know, western as hell. About a wagon train." As they were poised to leave, Dobe Carey recalled that Uncle Jack got in his characteristic "last word" to Stan. The director called out, "Thanks for coming over boys!" When they reached the door, Ford, with a mischievous gleam in his eye, added "Hey Jones! For Christsakes, don't write anything about cactus. You don't know a goddamned thing about cactus!"

After a few short months, Stan was running with the big boys. Nationally syndicated gossip columnist Hedda Hopper took note of Stan's new employer in a November 22, 1949, column:

> John Ford, on location at Moab, Utah, bought three songs from Stan Jones (who wrote "Riders in the Sky") for his picture *Wagon Master*. Ford took 219 people and 25 horses on location. And shooting in the village of 1440 people has proved a Christmas gift to the natives. John promptly hired 75 people and 70 horses to work in the picture.

A biographer of John Ford wrote that the director was so taken by Stan and his music that "the movie threatened to become a Stan Jones concert with accompanying visuals." Stan was invited to Moab about a week after the shooting had begun and "was out on the set and riding around on horseback much of the time."

It wasn't uncommon for Ford to haze newcomers to his film projects, but Stan had a free pass for *Wagon Master*. In fact, Ford's relaxed, even joyous, demeanor during the making of the film flummoxed all of the old hands who had worked with the cranky, unpredictable director on past movies. He loved the scenic environs of Moab, respected the pioneer heritage of the local Mormons he had hired as extras, and took full advantage of the wide,

Stan, Dobe Carey, and Ben Johnson on a promotional tour for *Wagon Master*. *Courtesy of Douglas B. Green*

bronze waters of the Colorado to stage harrowing river crossings by a rolling armada of covered wagons. Dobe Carey stated, "Uncle Jack always said *Wagon Master* was his favorite picture. The entire picture was done in a spirit of friendliness; every member of the company doing their best. One month of total unity and happiness—that was *Wagon Master*." Ford's rare ebullient moods never lasted, though, and Stan was destined to feel the sting of the director's famous ire on his subsequent film project.

In a mid-December column, Hedda Hopper featured Stan and his relationship with Ford once again, this time with a bit of "imaginative" biography of the Singing Ranger thrown in:

> Stan Jones of "Ghost Riders in the Sky" fame has written special songs
> and music for John Ford's "Wagon Master." Stan was a ranger in Death
> Valley for 12 years. He needed a new engine for his automobile, came to
> town and thought maybe he could sell a song or two for 10 or 15 bucks,
> with a bottle of beer thrown in. "Sky" has brought him over $100,000. I
> asked how long he'd been writing songs. "Well," said he, "my mother says

just about all my life." "Have you any more?" I asked. "I guess about a hundred," said he. "I tore up a lot. They took too long to put down." Jones was born in Douglas, Ariz. He's bought a home at Lake Tahoe where he and his wife are spending the holidays. Said he, "John Ford is just about the greatest guy I ever met." You can say that again.

By this stage of his whirlwind career, Stan had soldiered through innumerable interviews with every type of media outlet across the country and had been pointedly drilled in every exchange about how he had come up with the idea for "Ghost Riders in the Sky." Stan's retelling of the "Ghost Riders" saga assumed embellished, creative hues according to his mood. Savvy enough to feed the media's expectations for a biography that matched the lofty heights of his famous song, he merrily played the game. The prosaic reality of his upbringing by a single mother in a quiet Douglas neighborhood didn't appeal as a talking point during his countless exchanges with reporters.

Before heading to the Mexican Hat, Utah, location shoot for John Ford's next feature film, *Rio Grande*, Stan embarked on a pilgrimage to Douglas with Olive. It was his first return to the haunts of his youth since 1933. Tagged by the town's local paper, the *Douglas Daily Dispatch*, as the "Douglas Songwriter" who was "standing on the threshold of a motion picture career," his visit was described as "a quiet look around the scenes of his younger days and for a visit with old friends." Stan went by the Douglas High School and mingled with a handful of teachers who remembered him, including Principal George Bergfield, who had supplied the Navy Enlistment Office with a good review of his prior pupil's demeanor in the fall of 1934. Stan drove Olive out to the base of D Hill for a spin around the Rogers Ranch to view the locale of his inspiration for "Ghost Riders." On the way back into town, they stopped by the Calvary Cemetery, where Stan "regretfully reported" observing the headstones of many of his boyhood acquaintances. He took particular pleasure in showing Olive the handsome brick St. Stephen's Episcopal Church at the corner of Eleventh and D Streets, where, he bragged to the *Dispatch* reporter who covered his visit, "I once went six years to Sunday services without missing a Sunday at the church."

Douglas had grown during Stan's seventeen-year absence, and he predictably noted the paved streets that were dirt back in his day and all the new homes and businesses in town. For Douglas citizens, the great excitement in Stan's return was owed to the success of his song "Ghost Riders in the Sky" and the near mystical sway that it continued to hold over the American public. Stan reminisced to the *Dispatch* journalist about "the days when he learned to play the guitar from cowpokes on the neighboring ranches" and how "from them, too, he heard tales of the Old West." He then shared with his hometown audience what is perhaps the closest thing to the bare-boned truth of how he came by the inspiration for composing his immortal song. He allowed that it originated "from a legend he heard from an old timer, Capp Watts, who first told him the story of the cowboy destined someday to see the 'devil riders' who would tell him his time had come."

Stan's fidelity to his Arizona hometown was reflected in his dream to bring Hollywood to Douglas someday. The *Douglas Daily Dispatch* article chronicling Stan's return visit in 1950 stated, "Mr. Jones is now working for John Ford of Argosy-RKO Studios in California. He said that the studio at present has a picture in the 'talking stage' which might possibly be filmed in the Douglas area—'which I would very much like to see them do,' he added." Try as he might over the next twelve years, Stan's efforts never moved beyond the "talking stage." The landscape of his adolescent adventures in the borderlands continued to shape his art until the end of his life, and in a simple, candid moment Stan told the *Dispatch* reporter, "Most of my songs are taken from experience I had in and around Douglas as a boy."

In another interview, Stan's creative draw on his childhood memories kicked in and he claimed he had first heard the Ghost Riders legend as a nine-year-old boy while seated on the porch of the old Slaughter Ranch. "Texas" John Slaughter was one of the Old West legends Stan invoked as being woven into the fabric of his childhood. Slaughter, a notorious sheriff of Cochise County from 1887 through 1890, lived on an impressive well-watered border spread about sixteen miles east of Douglas and indeed was still alive and a parishioner at St. Stephen's Episcopal Church when Stan was young. It's unlikely, though, that Stan would have been "seated on the porch of the old Slaughter ranch" at the age of nine because by then Slaughter was infirm, living in an apartment in Douglas, and barely a year away from death. Stan's enthusiasm for his legendary old neighbor carried into his later career with The Walt Disney Company where he developed the idea for the *Texas John Slaughter* television series that ran on *Walt Disney Presents* in the late 1950s. The show opened with Stan's theme song featuring a no-nonsense chorus promising bad guys a long nap on Boot Hill if they chose to cross Sheriff Slaughter. He once slipped in another small fib about Slaughter to Disney himself, as Walt was on the air introducing Stan and his accompanying musicians, "You know, John Slaughter was at my christening." Much as Stan would have loved this to be true, the notion that Slaughter would make a special trip into town to witness the blessed arrival of Stanley Davis Jones into the Episcopal Church is unlikely.

The most poignant retelling of his childhood adventures that Stan repeatedly offered to the press involved growing up on his "father's ranch." Even back in 1948 when Stan was still a ranger, his good friend George Pipkin wrote in his column, "Desert Sands," for the *Trona Argonaut,* that Stan's father had practiced medicine in Tombstone. On top of being an eyewitness to the shoot-out at the O.K. Corral in 1881, Dr. Jones had purportedly escaped death at the hand of Billy the Kid after a shoving match between the two at a local saloon the year before. Stan undoubtedly slipped this colossal invention to Pipkin with a straight face, an early indication that he was prepared for the big time when he would stand in the glare of the public relations spotlight brought on by "Ghost Riders."

The national press first mentions his phantom pastoral childhood in the May 1949 article featuring "Ghost Riders" in *Newsweek*: "The words are written around an old Western legend which Jones says he first heard as a boy on his father's Nevada ranch."

Vaughn Monroe recorded a special promotional disc explaining the origins of the "Cowboy Legend." Monroe announces that, according to Stan Jones, he was "a cowhand on his father's ranch in California" when he first heard the story "based on an old Mexican and Spanish superstition."

In a radio interview conducted by Lloyd Perryman of the Sons of the Pioneers in 1950, Stan unveiled yet another version of his "inspiration" for "Ghost Riders":

STAN JONES: Well, the idea for "Riders in the Sky" came from an old Indian legend which was first told to me when I was about, oh, twelve years old.

LLOYD PERRYMAN: Oh?

STAN: Yup. On a ranch in southern Arizona, my home, I had been sent out to do a chore or two on the ranch—I saddled up a horse and took off. After I finished my work, it was beginning to blow up a storm and

not having a poncho along I decided to take an old path up over the
mountains, which was between me and the ranch house.

PERRYMAN: Huh huh—

STAN: I was trying to beat the rain of course.

PERRYMAN: Yeah—

STAN: Well, right up on top of the ridge I met an old cowpuncher, sorta a
weird old fella.

PERRYMAN: So he was just sittin' there looking up in the sky, huh?

STAN: Yeah, was I scared.

PERRYMAN: Oh, I woulda been myself!

STAN: So—when I got to him, without even turning his head to look at
me, he said, "Son, look up into the sky and you'll see the red-eyed cows
of the devil's herd." And I looked . . . and there was a peculiar cloud
formation which was being rimmed by heat lightning—I saw that
devil's herd.

PERRYMAN: And what happened then Stan?

STAN: Huh! You never saw a horse or a boy get down off a mountain as fast
in your life. (Audience laughter) And believe me I've never forgotten
the story.

PERRYMAN: Well, then was when you wrote the song, huh?

STAN: Hmmm—No, it was when I was stationed with the park rangers in
Death Valley. It was on my birthday and I happened to look up into the
sky and, well sir, I saw that same kind of cloud formation as I had way
back the other time and so it all came back to me…and I went inside,
and wrote the song.

The press wasn't the only target of Stan's talent for spinning tall tales. Dobe
Carey observed that about half of his good pal's stories "had a little wind behind them." One hundred mile per hour gales might be closer to the mark.
Stan, exhibiting his usual truth-stretching zeal, once told a friend that when
he was four or five years old at his family's Cochise County home he heard
"men talking out in the living room, smoking cigars." On the pretense of
getting a drink of water, he stuck his head in the door to see who was talking
to his father and, lo and behold, there sat Johnny Ringo and Wyatt Earp,
in a scene drawn straight from a Charlie Nichols melodrama. Comparable
whoppers persisted throughout Stan's career: he possessed a master's degree
in zoology from U.C. Berkeley, had met Pancho Villa in Agua Prieta as a

youngster, and had run away at the age of thirteen to join the *Beverly Hillbillies* radio show in Los Angeles only to be dragged back home by "the long arm of the old man." Some of these stories may have originated in the imaginations of inventive reporters, but Stan, as usual, was adept at slipping plenty of his own blarney to an eager, gullible press.

Stan's honeymoon with Ford extended into 1951 when the director asked him to compose songs for his next western, *Rio Grande*. Set to star John Wayne, the story revolved around a lieutenant colonel in the U.S. Cavalry who struggles to reconcile with his estranged wife and soldier-son while fighting Apaches along the southwestern borderlands. At Stan's suggestion, Ford had employed the Sons of the Pioneers to record Jones's songs written for the *Wagon Master* soundtrack, and now the preeminent western band was slated by the director to perform Stan's compositions in his new film, acting as the "The Regimental Singers." Ford's daughter, Barbara, had fallen for a member of the Pioneers, Ken Curtis (renowned as *Gunsmoke's* Festus later in his career), during the recording sessions and the two quickly became engaged, a fact meant to be kept secret until officially announced by the Ford family. Stan had been awarded a bit part as a sergeant in *Rio Grande,* but before the filming began, his garrulous nature had gotten the best of him and he let the news of the impending marriage slip. John Ford was furious. Dobe Carey wrote, "I had wondered how long Stan would manage to go unscathed by the wrath of Ford."

Ford's punishment was to refuse to speak to Stan directly for the duration of the filming. Carey recalled Ford's petulant tactics in dealing with the blabbermouth Jones:

> He'd notice Stan on the set, walk straight up to him, look him in the
> eye (you were never exactly sure about this, because of the eye patch
> and the dark glasses), and then call, "Dobe!" Over I'd come. "Yes, Uncle
> Jack?" Then Jack would say, "Ask *him* (he would not say his name) if he's
> rehearsed the songs with the Pioneers. The ones he wrote." Now the three
> of us are standing in a tight group. So I would say to Stan, feeling very
> foolish, "Have you rehearsed the songs with the Pioneers? The ones you
> wrote?" And Stan would say, "Yes, I have, and they sound great." Then

Ford would say, "What did he say?" And I would say, "He says, yes, he has, and they sound great." That's the way it went during the whole shooting of Rio Grande.

Stan managed to endure the rancor of John Ford on the set of *Rio Grande*. Luckily for him, Ford, renowned for the economical use of his resources, wrapped the picture after only thirty-two days of filming. One of the magical highlights of *Rio Grande* emerges when the Sons of the Pioneers softly croon Stan's song, "My Gal Is Purple," as John Wayne paces slowly along the river shore at sundown, torn between his sense of duty and the love he continues to harbor for his estranged wife, played by Maureen O'Hara. The song is a serene, poetic intonation of longing for a lover who is imagined to be lit somewhere in the shared twilight, glowing in the purplish penumbra of the gathering dusk.

Jones and Ford mended fences eventually, and Stan was welcomed back into the director's good graces. Even though Stan wouldn't work again professionally with Ford until 1955 when he was hired to write the theme song for *The Searchers*, the two remained members of a loose-knit gang of drinking buddies. Ford would often wander over to George O'Brien's place in Brentwood to stave off the restlessness he felt between film projects, and there he usually found a gaggle of his actor minions in a convivial mood "having a few." O'Brien's son, Darcy, recalled "one of my best memories" is "sitting around with Ford and Stan Jones and Dobe Carey at my father's place and having Stan Jones sing 'Riders in the Sky.'"

Publicity still from *Rio Grande:* Stan Jones surrounded by the Sons of the Pioneers, clockwise from top, Lloyd Perryman, Tommy Doss, Ken Curtis, Karl Farr, Hugh Farr, and Shug Fisher. *Courtesy Lilly Library, Indiana University, Bloomington, Indiana*

CHAPTER 12

SILVER SCREEN SONGWRITER

GENE AUTRY, EVER THE ASTUTE ENTREPRENEUR, ATTEMPTED TO RIDE the wave of "Ghost Rider's" popularity beyond 1949. Another song composed by Stan back in Death Valley, "Whirlwind," was included in the package for Autry put together by the William Morris Agency. Hedda Hopper continued to keep tabs on the Singing Ranger in her syndicated gossip column, writing in December 1950: "Gene Autry did it. Got Stan Jones who wrote 'Ghost Riders in the Sky,' to be in his next picture, 'Whirlwind.' Of course, Stan is writing a couple of songs for it." In the end Autry wound up singing only "Whirlwind" in the film and Stan's part in the movie turned out to be a brief uncredited appearance. The song itself is a lovely, evocative allusion to the whirling dust devils materializing out of nowhere to scamper across the desert floor of Death Valley. "Whirlwind" demonstrated Stan's natural gift for songwriting and signaled that he was not just a "one-hit wonder" after his big score with "Riders in the Sky."

Released in April of 1951, *Whirlwind* received a rather tepid response at the box office. At this stage in his career, Autry had recognized the growing power of television in America and was already shifting his sights to the small screen for his good guy/bad guy shoot 'em ups. Building on his work with John Ford, Stan continued to write songs for feature films, but he too would shift his creative focus to television by the mid-1950s.

Stan had never been content to rest on the laurels of "Ghost Riders," and he began to explore new avenues to utilize his artistic instincts. He had composed an operetta entitled *Legend of the Woodland Bells*, based around the idea of a "crew of rough, rugged lumberjacks and a little girl." Optioned to producer Aubrey Schenk at Universal in May of 1950, Stan's musical was never produced, but Schenk entertained visions of *Legend of the Woodland Bells* as a potential vehicle to introduce another "Shirley Temple" to the silver screen. Stan also gained permission in 1951 from Secretary of the Interior Oscar L. Chapman to utilize the "files of the rangers," hoping to mine his personal experience and affinity for the National Park Service to develop future projects for radio, television, and films.

In 1952, Stan began to collaborate occasionally with other songwriters, most notably with Russian émigré Dimitri Tiomkin. Tiomkin had enjoyed a long productive track record of creating successful film scores for projects directed by industry giants such as Frank Capra, Howard Hawks, and Alfred Hitchcock. He had just completed scoring the music and co-writing the theme song for *High Noon*, for which he would be awarded two Oscars in 1953. Jones wrote the lyrics and Tiomkin composed the music for the song "So Much To Me," written for *The Steel Trap*. Starring Joseph Cotton and Teresa Wright, the film portrayed the attempt by a banker to embezzle a million dollars from his employers and then flee for Brazil with all the loot. "So Much To Me," sung by jazz vocalist Helen Humes, drifts in and out of a scene set in New Orleans as the Joseph Cotton character struggles with his conscience while his loyal wife remains in the dark about her husband's heist. The lyrics and melody convey the appropriate melancholy mood. "So Much To Me" stands as the only non-western songwriting effort by Stan to make it to the big screen.

The duo produced a couple of other tunes, one named "Sweet Bread," sold to Gene Autry's producer for a film project that he was developing, and a song described as a "Kentucky folk tune," written for the Howard Hawks western, *The Big Sky*, that didn't make the cut in the final edit. The idea promoted by Zane Grey's son, Romer, of turning one of his father's books, *30,000 On The Hoof,* into a musical, with Stan and Dimitri Tiomkin providing the songs, was kicked around in the tabloids, but that project failed to get beyond the talking stage.

Stan landed a small part as "Sheriff Blake" in a low-budget western, *The Last Musketeer*, in early 1952 that starred Rex Allen and Slim Pickens. Shortly after that production wrapped up, he was hired to write a song for another B western, *The Rough, Tough West*. Released in June of 1952, it starred Charles Starrett in a dual role as sheriff of a mining town and his alter ego, the Durango Kid. The song that Stan wrote for this film, sung by the "Yodeling Blonde Bombshell," Carolina Cotton, was a sprightly tune titled "Cause I'm In Love." Backed by Bob Wills and the Texas Playboys, Cotton sang, "A shady lane, a passing train / The spider on the ceiling / Everything looks crazy / 'Cause I'm in love." The lines don't exactly rise to the imaginative heights of a Cole Porter couplet, but they showed off Stan's knack for hammering out a decent song.

Another forgettable western, *The Marshal's Daughter*, was released in June of 1953 and featured the title song written by Stan and sung by Tex Ritter. The lyrics are pure hokum, reflecting the cornball aspects of the screenplay he was given to work with. An artist can't produce a gem at will: Stan did what he was hired to do, and although he wrote his share of pedestrian lyrics, many of his songs written after 1950 continue to stand the test of time. However, even at this early stage in his Hollywood career, it was clear that he would forever be associated with "Ghost Riders." It was the exception, not the rule, when he was referenced in media releases solely as Stan Jones. He was "Stan Jones of 'Ghost Riders in the Sky' fame."

The Joneses settled into a semi-nomadic lifestyle, staying in Southern California while Stan engaged with his movie projects, and then heading up to their home at Crystal Bay on Lake Tahoe as his schedule allowed. They had a beautiful place right on the lake, entertaining friends and family as often as was practical. Dobe Carey recalled a journey that he and Ben Johnson made to visit Stan and Olive, describing a marvelously simple few days of "going out fishing on the lake and stuff." Keith Poehlmann, a nephew of Stan's, attended the University of Nevada at Reno and remembers his uncle's phone call inviting him up to Tahoe for the weekend. They drove together into Carson City on Saturday night, where Stan sang a couple of songs at a charity benefit. Stan's nephew wrote: "That weekend I really got to know Stan. He told me of his plans, hopes, and dreams, and two places he was in love with, Puerto Peñasco, a little fishing village on the Sea of Cortez and Sedona, Arizona, where he wanted to retire." Stan's sister, Jeanne Dubs, and her family journeyed to Crystal Bay for a visit. Her son, Bill Dubs, remembers

The Jones's at home at Crystal Bay on Lake Tahoe: left to right, Bill Dubs, Berta Jones (partially hidden), Stan Jones, and Olive Jones. *Courtesy of Bill Dubs*

his uncle's extensive knowledge of the geology of the Tahoe region, recalling, "Stan was a very bright guy." Bill also noted, "Stan was a heavy drinker and a heavy smoker. He and my dad drank a lot of whiskey together."

Despite the incriminating photo in *Life* magazine of Stan smoking and enjoying a beer back at the Emigrant Ranger Station, he received a hero's welcome in Olive's hometown of Preston, Idaho, on their first visit there after "Ghost Riders" hit the big time. A cousin of Olive's fondly recounted: "It was the talk of Preston and everyone was telling everyone of their connection to Olive and Stan and I for one was so proud—still today when I hear the song I have to tell whoever is with me that my cousin's husband wrote that song." Stan and Olive, along with a small entourage of friends and family, journeyed to the local dinner club, the Deer Cliff Inn, where word soon got out that the Singing Ranger was in the house. Olive's cousin was there and said, "Of course Stan had his guitar, and when folks saw him he could not escape singing his songs, and everyone loved him and his music."

While Stan had become fond of exaggerating the particulars of his boyhood biography, one aspect of his life he couldn't fudge was the fact that he remained supremely unaffected by all the hoopla that surrounded his breathtaking ascent into the public eye. A swell, affable guy to begin with, Stan remained the cheery optimist that he had been before success found him. "Stan could tell a good joke or a good story and make it stick," a nephew of his recalled, and "he always had a smile on his face. Stan and Olive loved and accepted everybody, and everybody was their friend." Johnny Western attests to his friend's demeanor: "He had that great grin all the time. You see most pictures of Stan and he's got that little kid's grin on his face. That's what I remember most about him; he was always an up guy."

Lloyd Perryman, duly impressed by Stan's remarkably keen intellect, recalled, "He had an extremely active mind. You had to know Stan for a while to realize how very brilliant he was. There was no subject you could find that Stan Jones wouldn't have a great knowledge about." Once, in a friendly attempt to stump Stan on a historical topic, Perryman and his wife consulted encyclopedias and checked out library books pertaining to the arrival of the conquistadors in Mexico. On Stan's weekly visit to their home, the Perrymans discovered that, "Stan knew everything we had learned . . . plus a good deal more!"

Stan was also supremely community-minded and made himself available in the Los Angeles area for fund-raising events, entertaining for such diverse causes as a benefit luncheon at a Junior Auxiliary Jewish Home for the Aged and a dinner celebrating the opening of a new Mickey Finn Youth Club, where three hundred underprivileged kids were served a Christmas holiday dinner. Dobe Carey, Stan, and a musician buddy of theirs, Frank Miller, grabbed their guitars and teamed up every Christmas vacation to visit and sing for the bed-bound military vets at the Santa Monica veteran's hospital.

As was the accepted custom in that era, drinking was a routine aspect of social intercourse. Dobe described the strategy that he, Frank, and Stan mapped out for their hospital holiday caroling: "We'd start out at a place I think was called the Broken Drum on Wilshire and Santa Monica and had a couple of belts, go out and sing for the guys in the hospital and then we'd come back and finish our drinking." Carey mused in his fine and frank autobiography, *Company of Heroes*, that perhaps he and his hard-drinking, happy-go-lucky pals were the "cause and inspiration for women's lib." He quoted lyrics written by Stan to frame his recollections of the errant behavior of his partying pals:

"Boots and Stetsons and sixguns and the lilies grow high. They grow for a man with a gun-slingin' hand who before his time must die. . ."

Those words are from a song called "The Lilies Grow High," written by my friend Stan Jones. I think those poetic words exemplify "prime time" of the 50s and early 60s. Stan was a dear friend and one of the many talented buddies I hung out with in those glory days. They were carefree, freewheeling days, and thinking back, selfish days on the part of us married guys with kids. We picked at our guitars and sang and drank with complete abandon. Our wives were present at a lot of those hoedowns, but they never had the freedom we did.

By all accounts, Stan and Olive were constant companions and devoted to one another, while enjoying a "wonderful" marriage. Olive, in her typically calm and understated manner, described her twenty-year relationship with her husband as "always a challenge and always interesting." According to Carey, Stan "drank all the time, but he never got in trouble with it." He remembered that when Stan and Olive were staying in a cottage behind his mother's place in the early 1950s, Stan would march into the kitchen of the main house in the morning and announce, "Well, I gotta go down and mix with the philistines." He'd pour himself a big shot of bourbon and "drain it down the hatch and off he'd go—that was at about 10:30 in the morning."

Olive's relaxed good humor contributed to her tolerance of the intemperate antics of her husband and his thirsty cohorts. Olive had joined Stan and Dobe on a location shoot for a Disney film in Clayton, Georgia, where, Dobe recalled, "everyone was stewed every night . . . except Olive." Sitting in the front row for a musical review that the cast was performing, Olive began to laugh hysterically when Carey mistakenly sang the word "sack" at the tail end of a line in one of Stan's songs written as, "Blow the whistle and clear the track." Carey looked down at Olive and his first thought registered that perhaps his fly was down, she was laughing so hard. "She teased me about that for years," he fondly remembered.

In April of 1953, Stan offered his talent to organize a "16-voice Ranger Choir" to participate in a patriotic public-service program to be recorded and then broadcast to American and United Nations' troops overseas on the Armed Forces Radio Service network. He continued to field offers to write songs for westerns, but as Hedda Hopper reported in a May 21 column, a song that he had already written inspired fledgling director and actor John Ireland to change the name of his new project:

> When John Ford returned from England recently, his pal, Stan Jones, who
> wrote "Ghost Riders in the Sky," gave a party for him and cracked out with
> a new tune, "Hannah Lee." John Ireland, who was present, decided he
> must have the song in his picture, "Outlaw Territory." So he got it. Final
> result was that the picture title was changed to "Hannah Lee."

Partly filmed with pioneering 3-D technology, *Hannah Lee: An American Primitive* turned out to be a minor disaster. Starring Macdonald Carey, John Ireland, and Ireland's wife, Joanne Dru, the film was roughly based on the life of lawman, outlaw, and assassin Tom Horn. This was to be Ireland's first and last directing experience, as the 3-D process was poorly managed and the resulting film was muddy. When the attempt was made to revert to 2-D, the color images remained blurred, forcing the producers to re-edit the film into black and white, rename it *Outlaw Territory*, and shorten it to an hour in length, fit only for television.

In contrast, Stan's energetic composition, sung by Ken Curtis in the original film, holds up remarkably well. Stan's protagonist in the song isn't about to take the heat for his lover shooting her husband point-blank and hang for it. The robust chorus of "Hannah Lee" portends the confession of the murderess and Ms. Lee winds up dangling from the end of a long rope.

Director John Sturges, whom Stan had first run across at Stovepipe Wells when he and his crew were ensconced in Death Valley back in 1948 to film *The Walking Hills*, lifted a tune that Stan had written for John Ford's *Rio Grande* entitled "Yellow Stripes." The song was slated for use in *Escape From Fort Bravo*, a Sturges film released in 1953, starring William Holden as a ruthless Union captain who lords over Fort Bravo, a prisoner of war camp full of Confederate soldiers itching to escape. Essentially a short military marching anthem, "Yellow Stripes" provided an excuse to use footage of a cavalry regiment riding in file either into or out of a U.S. Army fort with the troops robustly singing about their horses and their "gals"; in that order. "Yellow Stripes" is a deceptively simple, yet stirring songwriting effort by Stan that two renowned American directors found worthy enough to find a cinematic home for.

Stan next tackled songwriting chores for a pair of decidedly obscure films. The first, "In The Shadows of My Heart," was written for a B western released in the fall of 1954. Promos for the film *Jesse James' Women* featured the lurid tag line "Beauty vs. Beauty For The Love of Jesse James!" The lyrics, sung in both English and Spanish by a raven-haired actress playing a Mexican love interest of James, include the lines, "These shadows seem to taunt me / Deep in my very soul they haunt me / With memories of a stolen love we knew / No matter where upon this earth you stray / In the shadows of my heart you'll stay." Stan's work reflects the influence of his teaming with the seasoned composer Dimitri Tiomkin. "In The Shadows of My Heart" is a musically sophisticated and lyrically tender reflection of lost love, which briefly redeems an otherwise forgettable film.

The second was for another western in 1955 titled, *Tribute To A Bad Man*. Starring in one of his least memorable roles, James Cagney plays a tough horse rancher who's fond of stringing up rustlers. Stan's song, "Rough Wrangler," is used in a scene where the cantankerous rancher, with a bullet lodged in his back, swallows a few generous dollops of whiskey and orders his green sidekick to carve out the lead with a Bowie knife sterilized in a campfire. Cagney alternately grimaces and then mumbles the humdrum lyrics to Stan's song during the fireside procedure: "Oh I love my horses, my woman, my whiskey / And there's no better reason for living / Make love in the moonlight and hit the trail west."

Stan then turned his skills to an assignment by John Ford to write the theme song for his next film, *The Searchers*. The film is regarded as the greatest western that Ford ever directed, and Stan rose to the occasion and produced a song that stands with his finest post-"Ghost Riders" compositions. Sharing the movie's title, "The Searchers" artfully evoked the theme of a man caught in a web of violent revenge who then struggles to reconcile his wanderlust with his inbred sense of duty to his family. The first verse, sung by The Sons of the Pioneers over the opening credits, sets the restless tone of the film: "What makes a man to wander? / What makes a man to roam? / What makes a man leave bed and board / And turn his back on home? / Ride away . . . Ride away . . . Ride away."

In *The Searchers*, John Ford's stalwart leading man, John Wayne, portrays Ethan Edwards, an unapologetic Confederate soldier who visits his brother's family on the perilous Texas frontier after the Civil War has ended. Comanches slaughter most of the family after Ethan is called away, wracking him with guilt for not being on hand for the fight. Edwards then begins a relentless search for his young niece who has been taken captive by the Indians, ready to resort to any violent act necessary to avenge the loss of his kin. The final verse of the song, "A man will search his heart and soul / Go searchin' way out there / His peace of mind he knows he'll find / But where oh lord,

lord, where / Ride away," compellingly frames Ethan's dilemma at the end of the story when he faces the choice to ride back into the lawless frontier as a warrior or to seek the civilized comforts of hearth, home, and family.

Stan's best compositions were autobiographical. Writing from the heart of his experience, both "Ghost Riders" and "The Searchers" reflect the unrest in Stan's being as he wrestled with the tumult of his troubled, extended adolescence. He had stood on the same symbolic threshold that marked the crossroads for Ethan Edwards in *The Searchers*. Leaving behind the wreckage of his failed search for peace in his twenties, Stan made a fresh start and discovered the "peace of mind he knows he'll find" when he married his partner for life, Olive. Stan Jones had heard and taken to heart the "Riders" redemptive advice to "change your ways."

Except for one last call in 1959 from John Ford requesting a song for his film, *The Horse Soldiers*, Stan's freelancing days as a songwriter for movies had come to an end. By the middle of 1955 Jones had acquired a new boss: Walt Disney.

CHAPTER 13

I'M NO ACTOR

THE WALT DISNEY COMPANY HIRED DOBE CAREY TO PLAY HEAD RANCH hand Bill Barnett on "The Adventures of Spin and Marty," which was to air serially on the weekly *Mickey Mouse Club* show in the fall of 1955. The popular series chronicled the activities at the Triple R Ranch, a boys' summer camp where adolescent city slickers could learn how to handle a horse. Singing around the campfire was *de rigueur* for fledgling buckaroos in the 1950s, and who better than Stan Jones, of "Ghost Riders in the Sky" fame, to lead the young wranglers in song. On Carey's recommendation, Disney brought on the Singing Ranger to compose western-style chanteys for the hormonally challenged cowpokes. He played the character of Frank, whose main tasks around the ranch appeared to consist solely of grinning, singing, and strumming his guitar, a role that fit Stan to a tee. His rousing "Yipi-ay, Yipi-yi, Yipi-o'" chorus of the Triple R theme song continues to happily haunt many an aging baby boomer to this day.

Stan became involved with a couple of other Disney projects in 1956. Fess Parker, enjoying his star turn as Davy Crockett in the Disney serial of the same name, starred in *The Great Locomotive Chase*. Stan wrote a forgettable ditty for the movie, entitled "The Sons of Old Aunt Dinah," while playing a bit part as a Union soldier disguised as a Confederate. The beard that Stan grew for his role in the film gave him an uncanny resemblance to Ulysses S. Grant, a fact that wasn't lost on John Ford. He later invited Stan to contribute a song and play a small, uncredited role as the Union general in his 1959 film *The Horse Soldiers*.

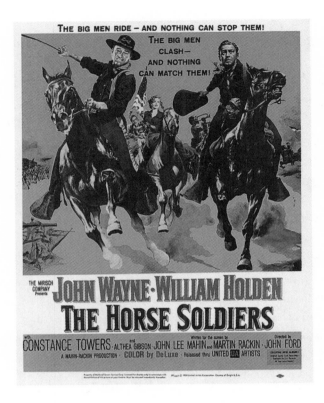

Stan's mother, who never lost her pride about her Confederate/Jefferson Davis bloodlines, was unimpressed by her son's Ulysses S. Grant appearance. When Stan visited Petaluma to see family while wearing the full beard for his job as an actor, Berta could barely stand to be observed at church with her hirsute offspring.

Stan also composed "Wringle Wrangle" for Fess Parker to sing in the Disney pioneer adventure *Westward Ho The Wagons!* A rollicking number that still sounds fresh today, "Wringle Wrangle" included lyrics that slyly stretched the Walt Disney dictums of decency with lines implying that a pioneer woman's work extended beyond the kitchen and into the bedroom.

At this point in Stan's career, he and Olive had grown weary of beating a path between their retreat in Lake Tahoe and their temporary series of residences in Los Angeles. They had been living in a house leased from Fred McMurray in Brentwood for many years. By the end of 1957, they had sold their Lake Tahoe getaway and found a house to buy in Tarzana near Gregory Peck, their friend from the days when he was in Death Valley filming *Yellow*

Sky. Situated on a verdant oak-shaded hillside that overlooked the San Fernando Valley, the rambling, white clapboard home on Casa Drive featured a large stone fireplace in a living room resembling the interior of an A-frame cabin with a high open loft on the upper story. In a matter of minutes, Stan could negotiate the hilly, winding streets down to Ventura Boulevard, a main thoroughfare that led to all pertinent destinations in the Los Angeles basin.

Olive shared the news in a letter to friends Allen and Shirley Reed in Phoenix: "Oh yes, just before Christmas we also moved into a new home and love it! It's in the hills—dogs, cats, and horses galore." The letter to the Reeds also contained an ominous report regarding Stan's health: "Things have been a little hectic for us of late—right after Christmas Stan went into the hospital for surgery, and has felt a little rugged. He seemed to be loaded with skin cancers, tumors and cysts, and he came out with plenty of scars—but now with a grizzled beard, he's on his feet again."

Gregory Peck had given Stan and Olive a large, whitish German shepherd that was fond of chasing cars. Stan put his Mount Rainier sign-making skills to practical use and hung a wooden notice at the entry gate below a miniature version of the Liberty Bell that read: "Our Boy loves cars in the road / Our Dog has a lousy sense of humor / Please keep the gate the hell closed / Ring Bell."

Stan stayed busy with creative endeavors beyond the scope of his Disney duties. He collaborated with an old songwriting pro, William Lava, to create a well-crafted and memorable theme song for the television western, *Cheyenne*. Stan also acted in a murder mystery entitled *Night Must Fall* as a member of the Brentwood Playhouse theater troupe, earning a rather prosaic review in the *Los Angeles Times*: "Stan Jones brought credence to the role of the inspector."

Then Francis Lyon, who directed Disney's 1956 *The Great Locomotive Chase*, took an interest in a couple of stories that Stan had written, and bought the rights for his production company to develop as film projects. One of them, titled *Two Miles East of Heaven*, was a modern western romance, while the other, based on a full length novel written by Stan, *The Lilies Grow High*, involved a feud between two brothers in Arizona Territory in 1885. Stan wrote three songs to accompany each story and the title song for *Lilies* stands today as a classic western gunfighter's lament.[1] Neither story ever saw the light

[1] Stan originally composed "The Lilies Grow High" in 1950 for a Twentieth Century Fox film to star Gregory Peck titled *The Gunfighter*. Apparently, Fox studio head Darryl Zanuck was unwilling to pay Stan a fair price for the song. According to a good friend of Stan's, the only times he had ever seen Stan angry was when Zanuck's name entered into a conversation.

of day as a motion picture under Lyon's direction, but Stan continued to hold out the fervent hope that *The Lilies Grow High* would one day be produced and filmed on location in and around his hometown of Douglas.

The closest that Stan Jones ever came to realizing this dream of a Hollywood production based in Douglas was when Mort Briskin of Desilu Productions agreed to develop an idea that Stan had pitched for a television show that dramatized the modern-day adventures of the sheriff of Cochise County, predictably titled *Sheriff of Cochise*. The actual Cochise County seat was in Bisbee, about thirty miles west of Douglas, but that was close enough to home for Stan's liking, even though the series was exclusively filmed in locations around Los Angeles. Originally touted in the press as being "based on the files of the sheriff's office in Arizona's Cochise County," the half-hour show starred John Bromfield, whose undistinguished career to that point had consisted of minor roles in TV westerns and the occasional feature film. Bromfield played Sheriff Frank Morgan, who "traveled his territory in a high-powered station wagon equipped with a two-way radio." Acting as Harry Olsen, his right-hand deputy, was none other than the Cochise County native himself, Stanley Davis Jones.

Stan's imaginative powers kicked into high gear in support of the project. He outdid himself with outlandish exaggerations that accompanied the promotional material offered to the press for the new show. Entertainment columnist Walter Ames of the *Los Angeles Times* reported:

> An interesting note on Bromfield's sidekick in the series, Stan Jones, is that the latter was actually born in Cochise County. His father was one of three families who founded the county. Some of the stories in the filmed TV series involve the same characters and incidents still fresh in Jones memory via story-telling sessions with his father. His mother carries arrowheads from 24 Indian arrows in her body as a constant reminder of the days of the Old West.

(Journalistic fact-checkers were clearly not in high demand back in 1956.)

It's likely that Stan concocted the arrowhead story to justify the lyrics of the patently cornball theme song that he had written for *Sheriff of Cochise*. The song included the lines "Where the arrows soar" (followed by the "whoosh, whoosh" of flying arrows sound effects), "And the six-guns roar" (bang! bang!), "In Cochise, Arizona!" Stan's effort didn't pass muster with the Desilu production team and was not used for the series. Stan's propensity to fall back on his favorite romantic cowboy and Indian fantasies just didn't work for the modern setting of the series.

Stan interviewed on a Phoenix television program while sporting his "Deputy Harry Olsen" garb from the television series *Sheriff of Cochise*. *Courtesy of Brent Reed*

Sheriff of Cochise marked the high point of Stan's career as an actor . . . such as it was. His chief accomplishment as an aspiring thespian centered on his ability to temper the mirthful glint in his eye for most of the time that he was in front of the camera. Stan made appearances in twenty-seven episodes over the first two seasons. Many of the scenes find him sitting at his desk in the office with Sheriff Morgan as the phone jangles with the revelation of a fresh criminal caper that sets the two into motion. Stan was given a handful of lines to deliver now and then, but never had a script that offered him the chance to blossom above the limitations of his "sidekick" character, which was probably just fine with him. Stan was his own, best objective critic when he declared, "I'm no actor, and I have the film to prove it."

Keeter Stuart, great-nephew of Stan Jones and grandson of Max and Nell Poehlmann, recalls the thrill of visiting "Uncle Stan" on the set of *Sheriff of Cochise* in Los Angeles as a six-year-old gunslinger. He came prepared:

I was wearing my cowboy boots, my cowboy hat, and my brand new Mattel "Fanner 50" cap pistols with genuine tooled leather gunbelt and holsters. When we arrived, the cast and crew were shooting some scenes, so my Dad and I watched them zooming around for awhile until it was break time. When Stan (Deputy Olsen) spotted me, he began to advance menacingly towards me, his gun hand at his side ready to draw. I met his steely gaze and stepped out into the dusty street to face him. Stan was fast, but he was no match for me and my Fanner 50s. I took him out . . . he was down.

Stan's one and only regular stint on a prime time TV show ended in 1958 when chief of Desilu Productions, Desi Arnaz, ordered the fictional locale of the show shifted from Bisbee to Tucson in Pima County and renamed as *U.S. Marshal.* Stan's association with the show was shifted behind the cameras, but not before the city of Douglas rewarded him for his role in shining the spotlight on his hometown. In conjunction with the annual Settlers Days Rodeo and Parade, Douglas mayor Henry Beumler officially declared Friday, March 29, 1957, as Stan Jones Day in Cochise County.

Stan, John Bromfield, and their smiling spouses arrived at the Bisbee-Douglas International Airport to a rousing "gun serenade" by the Junior Chamber of Commerce, when all twenty-five members simultaneously "discharged their shooting irons as the two men left the American Airlines plane at 9:45 p.m." Mayor Beumler and real-life Cochise County Sheriff, Jack Howard, were in the welcome party, and when the smoke had cleared, Stan was ceremoniously awarded a big copper key to the City of Douglas by the mayor. Sheriff Howard offered his official welcome to Jones and Bromfield "on behalf of the law in the county." After posed photos, wide grins, and backslaps all around, the television stars and their wives were escorted to "rodeo headquarters" at the grand old Gadsden Hotel in downtown Douglas where they were to spend the night.

Friday was officially Stan's day. After a morning visit with a few of his old boyhood friends, Stan, along with Bromfield, held court at assemblies at the local high school and junior high school, where "both men addressed students and Jones sang several western numbers to his own guitar accompaniment." They were then whisked off to the county seat of Bisbee for a series of radio interviews and a ceremony in Sheriff Jack Howard's office, where John Bromfield accepted a leather belt bearing a silver buckle emblazoned with the insignia of Cochise law enforcement authorities.

The next morning, the stars of *Sheriff of Cochise* rode as grand marshals of the Settlers Days Rodeo Parade, an eclectic caravan of borderlands Americana that included an equestrian square dance team; the local American

Stan addressing Douglas High School students on "Stan Jones Day."
Courtesy of Cochise County Historical Society

Legion Drum and Bugle Corps; Rafael Romero and his popular racing horse
El Relampago; high school marching bands; and Jinx Graham, rodeo clown,
with his horse, Freckles. The guests of honor were then ushered to a prominent box in the rodeo arena grandstands to enjoy the roping and riding
events, and finally trotted out once more at the Saturday night dinner and
dance gala held in the Hotel Gadsden lobby. A beard contest was held at
10:30 p.m., but, alas, Stan was clean-shaven at the time.

Stan, no stranger to the glare of the media spotlights, reveled in all the
hoopla on his behalf. He made a special pilgrimage to the house that he remembered as his boyhood home on Fourteenth Street. Stan still stubbornly
held on to the dream that he would return "home" someday with a film
company in tow. The *Douglas Daily Dispatch*, in an article previewing his arrival in town for the Settlers Days Rodeo and using copy obviously provided
by Stan, proclaimed:

Stan's first full length novel, *The Lilies Grow High*, pertaining to turn-of-
the-century Arizona, is being developed into a screen play at this time, and
will be shot as a motion picture around Douglas this fall.

Stan in front of the house at 946 14th Street where he lived for a few years as a boy.
Courtesy of Cochise County Historical Society

For his part, John Bromfield also enjoyed the accolades and all the attention. After enduring a fairly anonymous run in show business before assuming the role of Sheriff Frank Morgan, he confessed to the *Los Angeles Times*:

> About 40 million see 'Sheriff of Cochise' or 'U.S. Marshal' every week. I'd have to do about twenty-five pictures, major pictures, over a span of eight or nine years for enough people to see me in the theater who see me in one week on 'U.S. Marshal.'. . . The show is seen all over the world. Television is a fabulous medium.

After tabling tentative plans to produce a motion picture version of Stan's creation to be shot in Bisbee, Desilu cancelled *U.S. Marshal* after the 1958 season. By 1960, John Bromfield had retired from acting and established a new career as a commercial fisherman based out of Newport Beach, California.

While *Sheriff of Cochise* was at the height of its popularity in 1957, Walt Disney sensed an opportunity to cash in on Stan's limelight as Deputy Harry

Olsen. As early as 1956, with encouragement from a division of Walt Disney Studios, Disneyland Records, Stan began to focus more of his creative energies on a series of musical endeavors. His inherent weakness as a lead vocalist prohibited him from recording with a major label such as RCA or Columbia, yet the folks at Disney appreciated Stan's unique talents and were eager to capitalize on his weekly television appearance. Stan relished the chance to prove he could make a commercial breakthrough singing and recording his own material. The Singing Ranger's chance to test his musical mettle arose on his first album for Disneyland Records—*Creakin' Leather.*

CHAPTER 14

CREAKIN' LEATHER

CREAKIN' LEATHER, RECORDED IN THE SPRING OF 1957, TURNED OUT AS a jarring blend of cheesy, 1950s-style instrumental arrangements mixed with simpler tracks that featured Stan backed only by his tenor guitar. The collection offers keen insight into his strengths and weaknesses as a songwriter. The first four selections on side one of the album yield a revealing amalgam of Stan's creative talents.

The title song, "Creakin' Leather," kicks off with an adventurous three-four-time signature that rhythmically evokes a trudging, cranky string of mules heaving along a steep trail. Stan had done his time with pack animals, and the lyrics, "You dusty-rumped old buzzard bait / Your floppin' ears keep time / Your stink, your sweat, we ain't home yet / Got another hill to climb," reflect the exasperating love/hate relationship between a packer and his or her string of oftentimes ornery critters. Any honest mule-packer would be hard-pressed to argue with Stan's observation: "No one but fools / Can spend a happy day a-packin' mules." Stan had submitted a description of every song written for the album to utilize for the liner notes and for "Creakin' Leather" he dryly opined, "'Course I love mules, even though I hope to never see one again."

Following Stan's ode to mules is "Deep Water," a composition that is an anomaly in Stan's extensive song catalogue. It's reasonable to assume that while at sea during his short stint with the navy in 1935, he had written out the lyrics as a poem as he pined for his new wife Helen. Whether Stan was writing songs during that stage of his life remains a mystery. More closely

© Disney. Used by permission.

related in style to "Mean So Much To Me" and "In The Shadows of My Heart," the gracefully toned "Deep Water" opens and closes with the sound of waves lapping a shoreline. A spoken-word interlude during "Deep Water" shines light on the seafarer's inner turmoil as he struggles to find contentment: "Some distant horizon may call you / Escape and go and find a paradise so romantic / But it's only in your mind."

Next up is "Sedona, Arizona," an energetic but hopelessly corny song, whose lyrics vied with "Wringle Wrangle" (also on this album) to tweak the boundaries of Walt Disney's usually strict moral decorum. The song's raconteur hooks up with "sweet Leona" in Sedona, Arizona, and the sweethearts immediately proceed to "make heap big love 'mid the red cliffs and sage." The randy action rolls on into the second verse and the star-crossed lovebirds' amorous adventures continue: "Arm in arm we'll go walkin' and there won't be no talkin' / 'Cause we'll have things to do, reckon you know the rest." The children arrive, the years pass, but the home fires in their little cabin stay cheerily hot: "Tho' the kids may be a-cryin', I'll keep right on eyein' / Leona, sweet Leona, my wonderful wife."

After the busy arrangement of "Sedona, Arizona," "The Burro Lullaby" arrives as a soothing, welcome respite from the well-intentioned yet overly florid efforts of the Disney music producers. Stan was finally allowed the chance in a recording studio to do what he could do best—to simply sing his songs while playing his guitar. "The Burro Lullaby" remained Stan's personal favorite composition of the more than two hundred songs that he wrote during his lifetime. "Ghost Riders" brought fame and fortune, but for Stan, "The Burro Lullaby" embodied the days in Death Valley when he and Olive shared the deep peace of the immense starlit skies at Emigrant.

With soft strums of his four-string guitar tastefully setting the mood, Stan gently intones the wistful lullaby, "God is watching the whole night through / O'er four little burros and even you," in reverent tribute to his love for Olive, the splendor of the natural world, and the spiritual awe he held for the divine creation of all that he held dear. Although "The Burro Lullaby" may sound maudlin to many modern listeners, it's a song that transports us to the heart of the man who was Stanley Davis Jones. "Ghost Riders in the Sky" is the song that burned Stan's name into the annals of twentieth century American culture. "The Burro Lullaby" will forever abide as the key to the inner resonance of his soul.

Stan had been asked by the staff at the Disney Music Department to submit a biography along with the outline of his songs for *Creakin' Leather,* and he agreeably shoveled a fantastical load of bull their way. Stan's rambling type-written story begins: "Gentlemen: The following is a biog as requested, with regard to my years on this planet and the songs which inadvertently evolved because of it." He continues:

> I was born June 5, 1914, in Douglas, Arizona. Pancho Villa was raising all kinds of hell at the time two hundred yards away in Mexico. This bandit was a close friend of my father's and my mother still has a picture of Pancho holding me on top of his big, white stallion. Almost my entire youth was spent on a cattle ranch or around various ones. As my parents were very early pioneers in the Arizona territory, my family was quite

well-known and a great amount of influence was exerted on my behalf
when necessary. This accounted for my being able to spend a great deal of
time on the Apache reservation, and when I stomped off mad, as young
boys frequently will, they had me brought back from an extensive freight
train trip in the company of Jeff Davis, now known as King of the Hoboes.

Stan's narrative flows on in this stream of consciousness mode for four pages.
This was show business and he worked for Walt Disney; Stan was merely
conjuring his own personal Magic Kingdom, fashioning a frontierland
past populated with larger than life western heroes and a boyhood spent
in a stable, two-parent household on a cattle ranch. There were occasional
hints of reality woven into Stan's biographical fabrications; he mentions
Olive's surprise gift of the Martin guitar, his inspiration for "Ghost Riders"
as a boy in Douglas, the fact that he was the only one of his siblings without formal musical instruction, and how he was nearly suspended from his
Death Valley ranger job when he refused to kill burros. Alluding to his sudden rise to fame, Stan confessed, "I would still be a happy, carefree Ranger
but for an almost unbelievable change of circumstances which threw me
headlong into the entertainment industry." He included news of his two
children, Davis and Molly, from his first marriage: "My son has taken a little
vacation from UCLA at the precise suggestion of Uncle Sam, and is in the
Air Force Scientific Research in England. My daughter is forcing a young
grandparentship on me August of this year."

Just about everything else in Stan's "biog" is pure hooey and much of it
ended up on the album notes for *Creakin' Leather*. On the backside of the
cover, we learn Stan had "adventure as a 'pardner' since the day he was born
to the tune of Pancho Villa's guns." A master's degree in zoology he purportedly earned from the University of California at Berkeley is given brief
mention, and then we discover that Stan, who in reality was about as shy as
a rodeo bull, is sheepish about sharing his songwriting gifts:

> His love of animals and a life-long desire to be a U.S. Ranger took over
> at this point. He joined up. Then, riding under the stars on the lonely
> mountain and desert trails, between the bad-man battling and occasional
> rescues, he began to sing, and to write as he sang. It was in secret. The
> young ranger was embarrassed, not by his talent but by what it produced
> in a country of tough hombres—hundreds of tender songs and romantic
> verses he hid away in bureau drawers.

He hesitatingly obliged some strangers, though, one day in 1949,
when he was assigned to guide them on a movie location scouting trip.
They called for campfire music, listened to "Riders in the Sky," hired him
as a technical advisor, and bought the song to boot.

This apocryphal scenario of Stan singing "Ghost Riders" around the campfire for movie location scouts has lingered as the version that remains the
most quoted as to how "Ghost Riders" ostensibly made the leap from Death
Valley to Hollywood. The source for most, if not all, of the misinformation
about Stan Jones that exists throughout the Internet springs from the distil-
lation of Stan's cockeyed biography by the Disneyland Records staff in 1957.

Walt Disney did his best to help promote *Creakin' Leather* and teamed up
with *Arizona Highways* magazine to coincide the release of the album with
the magazine's October, 1957, issue, which was set to feature a photographic
tribute to Stan's compositions inspired by various Arizona landscapes. The
Arizona Highways writer and photographer responsible for the article, Allen
Reed, had also conveniently persuaded the governor of Arizona, Ernest W.
McFarland, to proclaim September 14, 1957, as Stan Jones Day throughout
Stan's home state.

The public relations machinery roared into gear and on September
fourth Disneyland Records sent a memo along with a copy of the magazine
and record album out to "all D.J.s and Record Librarians" in the state of
Arizona. The notice announced, "This is an opportunity to bring a great
amount of attention and publicity to Arizona and Stan Jones. Coupled
with the activity is the release of Disneyland Records new Stan Jones album
'Creakin' Leather.' Most of these original songs written by Stan have the
State of Arizona as their locale."

In anticipation of Stan's arrival the Friday evening before Stan Jones Day,
Reed managed to corral a friend who ran a boarding school up near Prescott
to bus a load of his students down to the Phoenix airport to serve as an
instant "Stan Jones Fan Club." As Stan stepped off the plane sporting his
Sheriff of Cochise duds, the cameras flashed as his youthful welcoming committee cheered and hoisted signs painted by Disney artists trumpeting the
names of Stan's more notable songs and waved banners declaring, "Welcome

Stan and Arizona governor Ernest W. McFarland. *Courtesy of Brent Reed*

Home Stan Jones," "Welcome To Our Favorite Deputy Sheriff Of Cochise,"
and "We Love Stan Jones Music." Governor McFarland was there to present
Stan with the official proclamation, designating Stan Jones Day in Arizona,
and Stan handed the governor a copy of *Creakin' Leather* personally auto-
graphed by Walt Disney.

Stan signing autographs for fans. *Courtesy of Brent Reed*

On Saturday, Stan made the obligatory rounds of Phoenix radio and television stations outfitted as Deputy Olsen, soaking in the media attention, which he always bore with aplomb and a good-humored smile. Stan returned to California and a few days after the fanfare had died down, Allen Reed wrote a personal letter of thanks to Walt Disney, ending with; "I'd like to see *Arizona Highways* circulation reach the one million per month mark and 'Creakin' Leather' break one million record sales. That is shooting high but at least I sincerely believe all we did in joint cooperation was surely one step in the right direction."

Stan and Olive enjoyed a happy result of the Arizona promotional blitz for *Creakin' Leather* by forming a close friendship with Allen Reed and his wife, Shirley. In the spring of 1957, the Joneses had journeyed together to Phoenix to meet with the Reeds to discuss the preliminary plans for the *Arizona Highways* tribute to Stan, and the two couples bonded immediately. The Reeds had property up in Sedona, the gorgeous red rock wonderland Stan had set in his sights as a place he and Olive might retire one day. As much as Stan still fantasized about returning "to the woods," he remained

Stan and fans ready to enjoy a cake decorated as a *Creakin' Leather* record album. *Courtesy of Brent Reed*

hog-tied to the Hollywood environs of the entertainment industry. Letters over the ensuing years to Allen Reed reveal a friendly, envious banter on Stan's part.

Stan sent a collection of songs for Reed to review in 1961 and in the accompanying note wrote: "I would go into a great deal of detail . . . extend this memo farther . . . describe virtues, etc. . . . but I never speak, converse with, or fraternize with people so fortunate, so lucky and so smug as to claim an address at SEDONA (by God!) ARIZONA. In the meantime, we will allow you to look down your noses at we poor peasants who cannot live in that 'unmentionable place.'" Stan never realized his dream of leaving Los Angeles for quieter pastures and still today, Olive Jones, at the prim age of 95, resides at the home she and her husband shared on Casa Drive in Tarzana.

Despite the best efforts of *Arizona Highways* and The Walt Disney Company, *Creakin' Leather* failed to make much of a commercial impact. The record- buying public was keyed into rock and roll by the late 1950s, and the Disneyland Records label wasn't pushing the envelope of current popular music trends, appealing primarily to adolescent listeners. Following the initial splash of the Stan Jones Day promotional efforts by Walt Disney Studios, Stan's album was assigned a lower priority compared to the corporate push for the newly remastered soundtracks from a number of classic Disney films, including *Fantasia*, *Lady and the Tramp*, and *Dumbo*, all released for the first time on vinyl beginning in 1957.

Undeterred by the failure of *Creakin' Leather* to sell a million copies, Stan turned to his next project, one that he had dreamed of ever since he was thrust "headlong into the entertainment industry." Still pining for the days when he wore "the uniform, the badge, and the insignia as a Ranger," Stan temporarily hung up his cowboy garb and donned once again the famous "flat hat" worn by National Park Service rangers. Building upon the core repertoire of songs he had written for his "Ranger Chorus" concerts earlier in the decade, he developed a combined spoken word and musical tribute to the Park Service—*Songs of the National Parks*.

CHAPTER 15

SONG OF THE TRAIL

ON A TOUR OF WESTERN NATIONAL PARKS IN THE SUMMER OF 1957 TO promote and gauge support for the *Songs of the National Parks* project, Stan stopped at Mount Rainier. At Longmire, he had dinner with park ranger Doug Evans, who lived with his family in the same cottage where Stan and Olive had resided almost ten years earlier. Evans recalled Stan's enthusiasm for the album and how he described that he'd "written songs about the parks and park rangers, and that it would be soon released by Disney." Stan had also kidded Doug about his desire to switch jobs to become a park naturalist, good-naturedly teasing him as a "butterfly wrangler" and a "posy picker."

The next day on his way back down the mountain, Stan did what he loved to do and stopped by the Columbia Crest grade school to perform for the kids there. One student, Rhoda Pappajohn, who was in sixth grade at the time, remembers how Stan taught them the words to "Ghost Riders" for a sing-along, signed autograph books, and reminisced about his time at Mount Rainier. "It was a very special assembly for all of us," she said, "and to this day, I remember how very special it was to me."

Ranger Evans keenly anticipated the arrival of the promised "forest ranger" album and many months later, after it had failed to show, he wrote a letter to Stan inquiring about the project's status. The folks at Disney apparently didn't share Stan's eagerness to release the record right away, and according to Evans, "Stan took my letter to the Disney people and said . . . look, people are clamoring for my album!" The Walt Disney Music Company finally released *Songs of the National Parks* in mid-1958.

Stan, flanked by Daniel and Suzan Evans, during his visit with the Evans family at Longmire. *Courtesy of Doug Evans*

Photographs of the Grand Canyon paired with Old Faithful in Yellowstone graced the cover along with the official arrowhead insignia of the National Park Service emblazoned in the lower right corner. Prominently billed under the title is "Stan Jones and the Ranger Chorus," while on the flip side of the cover we learn that although the narration, words, and music are written by Stan, the fellow who actually performs the narration on the album is the vocal pro Thurl Ravenscroft, whose deep and preposterously resonant voice is best remembered as the original Tony the Tiger's in Kellogg's Frosted Flakes ads exclaiming, "Theeeeeyyy'rrrrrrree Great!"

On the back of the album underneath the head shot of a smiling Stan Jones in full-dress Park Service uniform, the text reads:

> Once in a while a man comes along who personifies a breed which is fast
> becoming a legend—the true, outdoor Westerner; rugged, sincere, sensitive
> and humble. Such a man is Stan Jones, logger, miner, cowpoke, railroader,
> sailor, National Park Ranger, dreamer, writer and creator of songs.

In contrast to the exaggerated renderings of the Singing Ranger's biography that abounded in the popular press (most originating from the bull-slinging master himself), the staff writers at Disney assigned to write the copy for *Songs of the National Parks* had actually pegged Stan's résumé and personality with a fair degree of accuracy. Clearly a dreamer extraordinaire, he had also remained a naturally warm, unaffected, and self-effacing man, who had used to exceptional advantage his natural creative talents to depict his world in words and song. As to the variety of vocations noted in the album copy, Stan probably had at least dabbled in all of the professions named, although the only record that exists of Stan as a "railroader" are the scenes of him with his General Grant beard behind the controls of a steam engine for *The Great Locomotive Chase*. Nonetheless, it was The Walt Disney Company's job to build Stan's image as a "legend" to match the majesty of the landscapes that he rhapsodized about in his honest effort to convey his abiding love for America's national parks and his respect for National Park Service rangers.

Described in the text as being "recorded at the request of the Department of the Interior," the back of the album featured a "Message from the Director of the National Park Service," Conrad Wirth:

> The music of Stan Jones, a former National Park Service Ranger, catches fleeting reflections from the western National Parks: Trails that reach from quiet woodland to windy mountain pass; the vastness and variety of Yellowstone, where the National Park idea began; chromatic landscapes of the Southwest culminating in the depths and distances of the Grand Canyon; expanding horizons revealed from Alpine summits; the busy approach of park visitors anticipating the charm of the wilderness; men of the mountains and forests; and the ranger dedicated to the perpetuation of this heritage for the benefit of future generations.
>
> Our National Parks are an investment in physical, mental, and spiritual well being, in something as simple yet as profound as good citizenship. Love of the land, pride in the American way and faith in the nation's destiny are their products.

The Ranger Chorus included the voices of Lloyd Perryman and other members of the Sons of the Pioneers, joined by a women's choir alternately chanting and singing the hymn-like melodies composed by Stan to glorify the western lands that he worshipped. The influence of his days "carrying the cross" at St. Stephen's church as a boy in Douglas are reflected throughout the album. Stan had occasionally woven religious themes into his songs, exemplified by the cowboy's choice between a righteous life and the ways of the devil in "Ghost Riders," but the influence of his faith is especially pronounced in *Songs of the National Parks*, featuring ecclesiastical passages of dialogue and lyrics that would have prompted the Reverend Simonson to smile from the heavens.

Stan as Wilson Brown on the set of *The Great Locomotive Chase*.
© *1956 Disney. Used by permission.*

The album commences with a narration packed with poetic images of the natural landscapes that encompass the national parks. Following are tracks titled "Grand Canyon," "Sons of the Mountains," "The Desert," "Along The Yellowstone," "Woodsman's Prayer," and "Rangers' Hymn." In one telling couplet from the tune with the most melodic zing of the collection, "Song of The Trail," Stan sums up his core spiritual beliefs: "I have seen the burst of glory and I've felt the mighty hand / Of the one who made all this out here and made

me what I am." Finally, after a stirring summation of the wondrous encounters with nature that may be experienced at our national parks, the narrative wraps up with: "This is our heritage, loaned to us by Almighty God."

Songs of the National Parks was Stan's heartfelt homage to the brief but hallowed years that he and Olive spent together living in the awe-inspiring surroundings of both Mount Rainier and Death Valley. In an August, 1958, letter composed by Stan, touting the album to bookstore partners at Park Service units across the nation, he wrote:

> I, personally, may or may not be known to you. I removed the uniform, the badge and the insignia as a Ranger some nine years ago this month. I have done many things and been many places, but I still find in my own heart that I really never have disassociated myself with the Service.

To modern ears, *Songs of the National Parks* seems an overwhelmingly schmaltzy period piece, yet for all the sermonizing and mawkish overtones, Stan's unique brand of sincerity shines through. This was a man who clearly relished his days of wearing "the uniform, the badge, and the insignia as a ranger." Stan wasn't one to forget his friends, and soon after the release of the album he sent a signed copy off to Mount Rainier: "To: Doug Evans and family—Thanks to you and your kind this all came about, and we all thank you." The Singing Ranger signed off with the sly counsel: "And be a good naturalist. Stan Jones."

Stan had enjoyed considerable success as a songwriter by any standard, but toward the end of the 1950s the niche for his unique brand of nostalgic western compositions had narrowed considerably. Although *Gunsmoke, Wagon Train, Have Gun Will Travel,* and a number of other television westerns were all the rage at the time, The Walt Disney Company provided the only real avenue for Stan to share the songs he had created over his lifetime that chronicled his romantic visions of the "Old West." Stan had retained enough credibility with the Disney team to promote the idea for the *Texas John Slaughter* series that developed and aired as part of the weekly *Wonderful World of Disney* show beginning in 1958. Stan was then awarded one last recording project, which the folks at Disney hoped might capitalize on America's stubborn fascination with the bygone cowboy and Indian era, to be titled *This Was The West.*

Released in March of 1959, *This Was The West* was a blend of the scattershot collection of songs on *Creakin' Leather* and the spoken word aspects of *Songs of the National Parks.* Sprinkled throughout the recording, though, were Stan's finest creative compositions beyond "Ghost Riders." Designed as a concept album that reflected Stan's panoramic take on the history of the American West, it included artwork by the Jones's good friend Shirley Reed and extensive liner notes written by Stan for each individual song bearing titles like, "Sacajawea," " Ol' Kit Carson," "Jim Marshall's Nugget," "Indian Spirit Chant," and "Songs of the Dance Hall Girls." The historical narratives were composed with the sincere earnestness of a wide-eyed teenager attempting to capture the past through the prism of a dime-store western. Stan's final paragraphs of text encapsulate his vision of the role he persisted in playing to rehash rose-colored accounts of the Old West:

> This, then, was the West. From Sacajawea to World War I, an era gone. It's an age as dead as the time of the Pharoahs, but it will be remembered as long as there is a fiction writer, a movie producer or a songwriter left on this earth . . . particularly by the young in heart, to whom the cowboy and the Indian, the buffalo and the gunman, the burro and the prospector are just as important as breakfast tomorrow morning.
>
> Even as Sputniks and satellites glide over the Western plains, signifying the years ahead and the unknown future, harken back to a glorious century and a romantic epoch in the history of mankind. Think back and remember . . . this *was* the West.

This Was The West also included "Rollin' Dust," "Wagons West," and "Yellow Stripes," songs recycled from the John Ford films *Wagon Master* and *Rio Grande.* The sessions for the album also afforded Stan the opportunity to record "Cowpoke" and "The Lilies Grow High," two superb songs that had languished for years without much public exposure. Stan also composed a batch of new tunes specifically for the album, and a rousing hallelujah-style gospel number titled "Saddle Up" was far and away the finest of the new bunch. Recognized by the Disney music gurus as a potential hit, "Saddle Up" was the only selection on the album not sung by Stan and instead entrusted to the golden-throated Thurl Ravenscroft, who rips through the exhilarating arrangement in high style, fronting a full-blown brass orchestra augmented by inspired backing vocals from a choir featuring the Sons of the Pioneers.

The lyrics reveal the blast of the archangel Gabriel's horn, announcing the occasion for all the marquee desperadoes and Indian chiefs, Billy The Kid, Jesse James, and Geronimo included, to gather and queue up to be assessed for entrance through the "golden gate." This will be a nonviolent crowd, for guns are turned in at the door before being called to face sentencing on judgment day. Stan just so happens to have a convenient alternative for those who don't make the grade for the trip to heaven: a doomed passage to an eternity with the ghost riders, chasing the devil's herd across the endless skies.

Typical of many artists, Stan doggedly believed that his best work lay ahead of him, but there was no way that he would ever rise above the pinnacle of "Ghost Riders in the Sky." It's not hard to envision a resigned smile and a knowing shake of the songwriter's head as he surrendered to the timeless power of his one truly great song, weaving it artfully into "Saddle Up" as the consummate metaphor for frontier hell.

"Saddle Up" turned out to be the last exceptional song written by Stan, and it is still covered occasionally by vocally adventurous Sons of the Pioneers-style western bands. The original recording is credited to both "Stan Jones and Thurl Ravenscroft," and it shows up on Disney music anthologies, sharing the spotlight with wide-ranging assortments of a few of Walt's old chestnuts including Fess Parker's rendition of "Wringle Wrangle," Annette Funicello's "Beach Party Tonite," and "Lavender Blue, Dilly Dilly" sung by Burl Ives. *This Was The West* shared the anemic commercial fate of *Creakin' Leather,* and although Stan would continue to sporadically work as an actor for The Walt Disney Studios through 1961, his days of recording for Disneyland Records were over.

CHAPTER 16

ROLL ALONG

STAN WASN'T A MAN TO GAUGE HIS PERSONAL WELL-BEING BY THE relative success or failure of any movie or musical project in which he was involved. He remained a happy-go-lucky guy who stayed busy and engaged with family affairs, charity efforts, researching book projects, working on western-themed short stories or poetry, and playing the occasional bit parts in television or film offered him by Disney. He manned a ham radio set from his Tarzana home, the hobby he had picked up along with his old Douglas buddies, Wayne Hester and John Rogers. Harold Poehlmann, son of Stan's older sister Nell and her husband Max, was living in Mexico in the late 1950s and recalls many nighttime airwave conversations with his illustrious uncle. Harold also fondly remembered family holiday gatherings in Petaluma when Stan, with his ever-present guitar, would delight the younger children of the household by surreptitiously noodling a few notes on it, then feign total surprise, and wonder out loud, "Who in the heck could have made those sounds?"

Stan remained in touch with a few old pals from his park ranger days. When he heard that Mount Rainier heavy equipment operator, Bud Molinek, was in the hospital at Ft. Lewis, Washington, Stan telegrammed: "Get off your back you turtle—You and I have done better than this—I don't know what you're trying to prove but you don't have to—You did that fifteen years ago—Get off it Bud there are lots more trails. Stan Jones." Molinek had hitchhiked from Mount Rainier down to visit Stan and Olive when they lived in Death Valley and he told the story to his daughter of how he "walked" across the desert to get to Emigrant. A motorist had stopped for Molinek to take him the last few miles down the highway toward Stan's ranger station and asked, "Hey buddy, don't you know it's 110 degrees out there?" Bud cheerily replied, "With the wind-chill it only feels like 90!" He and Stan were birds of a feather and Molinek's daughter recalled that they would "spend hours together, singing and spinning tales."

In 1959, Stan got a call from a young woman who claimed to be his daughter. During the process of applying for a passport and acquiring her birth certificate, twenty-five-year-old Jeanie Clarke discovered that she had been adopted at birth. Her adoptive parents agreed to help her track down her genetic father and the trail led to a "cowboy singer" in Los Angeles named Stan Jones. Jeanie called him and Stan agreed to meet her at a western bar in Hollywood. Sure enough, the pre-cowboy-change-your-ways-days had come back to haunt Stan. This was the child he had unknowingly conceived with his fifteen-year-old Mormon acquaintance back in March of 1934, just before he'd left Los Angeles to work at the gold mine on the American River. Stan cowboyed up: he drove his firstborn daughter to the Tarzana house to meet Olive.

Olive's generous spirit and acceptance of her husband's foibles is legendary among the many friends and family members who were privy to the Jones's inner circle. After recovering from the initial shock, Olive welcomed Stan's daughter into her home. In the ensuing years, Jeanie's husband and children were also embraced by Olive and Stan as full members of the extended Jones clan.

One of Jeanie's daughters, Anne Barrett, remembers visiting Tarzana at least a half-dozen times before Stan passed away. She and her siblings were instructed to call their grandfather "Uncle Stan" and learned the real nature of their connection to him only many years after he'd died. On one visit, she remembered a relaxed scene with her brother and sister in the living room by the fireplace, while all the adults were chatting in the kitchen:

> I was using my fingers to sketch a large horse into the nap of the
> cream-colored carpet; my younger siblings were quietly coloring nearby.
> I was engrossed in my project but have a dim recollection that the adults
> were talking about Stan's work and the props he used for it. At one point

Stan brought out a shiny revolver, and despite Olive's remonstrations, calmly fired a blank shot into the fireplace. I recall my father being uncharacteristically quiet while my mother seemed stunned. The dog had a bad case of the shakes. It was the loudest thing I had ever experienced. Olive seemed embarrassed and gave Stan a "well, you've gone and done it now" wave of the hand. Stan patted and spoke to the dog until it settled.

The appearance at the front door of Tarzana police officers called to the sound of a gunshot added to the drama of Anne's memory of the "thrilling" event.

Stan's great-nephew, Keeter, who had gunned down Deputy Olsen on the set of *Sheriff of Cochise*, recalled a similar performance by his uncle for visiting family members:

Sometime around 1960 we were visiting Stan and Olive at their house in Tarzana. This was a rambling ranch-style house with a huge (to my eyes) stone fireplace in the living room. My folks and several others were gathered at the kitchen adjacent to the living room. Suddenly Stan appeared at my side in front of the fireplace carrying a big pistol and handed it to me. It was heavy . . . the real thing. He said, "Shoot it into the fireplace." I must have looked rather puzzled at that suggestion, so he said, "Go ahead and shoot, it'll be fine . . ." Well, I needed no further urging. Now, I didn't know he had loaded the gun with blanks, but blanks or no, that first shot I fired was LOUD! I got one more shot off before the shocked folks in the kitchen ran into the room. They must have been amazed to see this young boy holding a smoking pistol while his grown-up great-uncle looked on, laughing uproariously at my grinning and their momentarily horrified faces. Stan was enjoying every minute of the show he put on.

Although Stan seemed to be bulletproof when it came to his cowboy pranks, simply growing facial hair got him back in hot water with his mother. On a Christmas visit to Petaluma in 1959, Stan was in the process of growing back his dreaded beard, this time for his minor role as Ulysses S. Grant in John Ford's *The Horse Soldiers*. Berta swallowed her chagrin at her son's role playing a Union general and reluctantly agreed to be seen in church once again with her hairy son, trusting that the three-year gap since Stan's last bearded visit had faded from her fellow parishioners' judgmental memories.

The happiest possible news for the Joneses in 1959 arrived with word that Olive was pregnant. Stan and Olive's friends the Reeds had just celebrated the arrival of their new son Brent and in a congratulatory letter sent by Olive in early January 1960, she wrote of her own thrill at her impending motherhood: "After waiting 17 years, I can't wait until the middle of next month. Will let you know all about the new arrival. Just think, if it's a girl maybe she will grow up and marry your new son and both of them could live in Sedona." This reference to Sedona was undoubtedly prompted by Stan's appearance as Olive was composing her letter. Olive wrote, "Stan just walked into the room and said how much he wishes we were living in your end of the country. With the new baby coming on, I sanction it. Who would want to raise a child in Hollywood."[1]

Olive gave birth to a baby boy, Stan Jones Jr., on February 19, 1960. In March, she penned a note to the Reeds: "I can't wait for you to meet the new baby and I'm anxious to meet your Brent. For an "ole" gal [Olive was forty-one when her son was born] and ex-school teacher I must admit I'm having one great time. Yes—you're right Shirley—it's all worth it. I never realized how much I had really missed."

Not nearly as genteel as his Mormon-bred wife, a letter sent by Stan to Allen Reed suggests: "Our very best to your new son. Perhaps we can encourage our boys to fight some time next year."

Stan sported a furry pair of muttonchop whiskers for his role as Seneca Howland in the Walt Disney adventure, *Ten Who Dared*. The film, released in 1960, documented John Wesley Powell's perilous 1869 attempt to navigate the Colorado River through the Grand Canyon with ten men in four wooden boats. Featuring a stellar cast that included Ben Johnson, James Drury, and Brian Keith, most of the dramatic sequences were shot along the Colorado River near Moab, Utah. The Drury and Johnson characters carried bad blood from being on the opposite sides of the Civil War.

In a scene set around the evening campfire, the tension is eased between the protagonists as they harmonize on a song, written by Stan, titled "Roll Along." Pronounced as "an old Southern tune," the two actors hesitantly join in, singing the words that poetically evoke the merging of a river into the sea as a symbol of the shared fate of all humankind. It's a moving and beautiful

---

[1] Stan Jr. was in fact successfully raised in Hollywood and today is an Emmy Award–winning music editor for films and television.

composition that resonates as a deeply authentic "old" song. Stan's creative juices continued to flow undiminished. During the scene, he plucks gently at his tenor guitar while his face, flickered by firelight, glows with the happy eye shine that he never quite learned to suppress in the presence of a rolling 35mm camera.

James Drury remembers Stan Jones as a "wonderful man," who worked cheerfully and effectively with everyone on the *Ten Who Dared* set. For fifty years after the making of the film, though, Drury erroneously believed he had nearly killed the wonderful man who had written "Ghost Riders in the Sky." Every evening after the Moab shoot, the cast and crew gathered to eat and drink (not necessarily in that order) at Scovill's, a restaurant owned by local justice of the peace, Ray Scovill. Drury, arriving back at his hotel one evening "well lubricated," inadvisably began to fiddle with a loaded .357 Magnum, precipitating an "unintended discharge" of the gun that sent a bullet through the wall, headboard, mattress, and into the floor of the adjoining room where "Jones was bunked." Drury had mixed up which Jones was bunked next door. At an awards ceremony in 2011, Drury was surprised to learn from the lucky survivor himself that it was not Stan Jones, but another member of the cast, character actor L. Q. Jones, he had nearly dispatched by mistake.

Arriving fresh from the rigors of his cinematic adventure through the Grand Canyon in *Ten Who Dared*, Stan created a small-town frenzy on a Thanksgiving visit to Petaluma in 1960. One might have assumed from the advance press notices in the *Petaluma Argus Courier* that the Singing Ranger had just starred in *Gone With The Wind*. The city fathers announced Stan Jones Day and laid out the red carpet, welcoming "one of the greatest talents in the field of entertainment." An event was held at the Little Hill Restaurant, where Stan, Olive, and their traveling secretary, Patricia Charles, were feted by "four of Petaluma's greatest ambassadors of goodwill," the Roostaires, a resident barbershop quartet. Despite a heavy rainstorm, the evening proceedings were attended by a "larger turnout than expected" and after "the star premier dinner," the assembled crowd journeyed to the nearby State Theater for a special showing of *Ten Who Dared*. Stan obliged his fans at the theater with a performance of a few of his best-known songs, following a short command appearance by the Roostaires.

The promotional blurb in the *Argus Courier* announcing the arrival of the adopted hometown boy who wrote "Ghost Riders in the Sky" featured a touching photograph of Stan that had been taken by The Walt Disney Company for the back cover of *This Was The West*. His ranger-style cowboy hat in the photo is slightly pushed up toward the top of his head to frame his full, round face, revealing a contented grin and his twinkling set of perpetually happy eyes that convey a man fully at peace with himself. Ever the dreamer though, Stan had let slip to the columnist who was covering his visit to Petaluma that *The Lilies Grow High* was "currently in screen preparation" and that a television series written by Stan on the U.S. park rangers was also in the works.

Stan boasted of another potential iron in the fire, one that the article reviewing his activities in Petaluma revealed under the heading "The Big Scoop about Jones":

> Later that evening Stan Jones said, "I have a scoop for you," and he
> then revealed that just before leaving for Petaluma he had a long phone
> conversation with a man in Moscow who turned out to be Premier Nikita
> Khrushchev, and as a result of this conversation, the U.S. State Depart-
> ment will sponsor Stan Jones and his choral group on a tour of Russia,
> where they will do the authentic history of the American West, with words
> and music by our own Stan Jones.

There is no record of "Stan Jones and the Ranger Chorus" having ventured off behind the Iron Curtain and a personal phone conversation between Stan and Khrushchev defies belief. Whether Stan's hopes for a new TV series based on his experience with the National Park Service or a film version of *Lilies* ever had any substance is also unknown. In either case neither ever materialized.

In the fall of 1960, Stan gladly thrust himself into the middle of a controversial battle over the coyotes that howled and roamed in the wilds of the Hollywood hillsides. Opportunistically foraging in pet owners' backyards, a coyote would feast every now and then on a family's cat or dog. Always quick to stand up for his four-legged brethren, Stan dutifully appeared at a public hearing before the Animal Regulation Commission convened to determine whether or not a trapping permit would be issued to put a dent in the suburban coyote population. Labeled by a *Los Angeles Times* reporter as "a songwriter who composed 'Ghost Riders in the Sky'" and who spent "15 years as a ranger-naturalist in national parks," Stan testified in response to a trapper's contention that leghold devices using plastic-protected jaws would not injure the animals and would humanely hold them until they could be shot: "There isn't a trap or poison made which won't cause suffering to the animals." He added, "One coyote will kill up to 100 gophers, ground squirrels, rats, or moles a week and a rattlesnake is a great delicacy." Stan couldn't resist injecting a little humor into the proceedings as the *Times* reported:

> Jones, in closing, said that the protesting residents erred in blaming coyotes for loud howls in the night. "The barking is that of dogs," he said. "Coyotes only give two or three yelps and those are in the key of D flat."

The trapping solution was eventually scrapped and the balance of nature continued to teeter onward in Stan's semi-wild Tarzana neighborhood. The following year, Stan was handed symbolic lawful reign over his shady Los Angeles suburb when the city awarded him the title of Honorary Sheriff of Tarzana.

Stan continued to be engaged in a number of varied projects. He played a role in a production by the Brentwood Playhouse of Somerset Maugham's play, *Jack Straw,* which generated funds for a donation to the City of Hope charity. Along with his pal, Dobe Carey, and a host of other TV "horse opry" personalities, he entertained the participants of an Easter egg roll, held at the Beverly Hilton Hotel, which was sponsored by the Pinafores organization to benefit the League of Crippled Children. Joining forces with composer-conductor Carmen Dragon, Stan wrote the lyrics to a musical play titled *We Believe* that served as the grand finale for a tribute commemorating Public Schools Week performed at the Santa Monica Civic Auditorium. Dragon also served as the music director for a weekly educational radio program beamed to elementary school students throughout the western United States, *The Standard School Broadcast*. He invited Stan to create a series of vignettes on the history of the American West to be set to music for the program, a request right up the Singing Ranger's alley. The album titled *I Am An American* was released in 1962 and turned out to be Stan's final recording project.

During this period Stan was slowly winding down his relationship with The Walt Disney Studios. After his role as guitar-carrying Seneca Howland in *Ten Who Dared*, the studio cast him for the last time, playing the character Doc Slocum for a few episodes of the *Daniel Boone* serial that ran on *Disney's Wonderful World of Color* in 1960 and 1961. Stan warrants his own biography on *The Original Mickey Mouse Club* show website and, under

Stan on the set of *The Adventures of Spin and Marty,* a segment of *The Mickey Mouse Club* at the Golden Oaks Ranch. © *Disney. Used by permission.*

the heading of "Songwriter and Serial Actor," the summation of his years at Disney read:

A former rodeo cowboy, miner, logger, firefighter, and park ranger, turned songwriter and sometime actor, Stan Jones worked off and on at Disney from 1955 up to his death. Even longtime fans of the first Spin and Marty serial find it hard to recall him having any lines in it, though his songs would be used for all three seasons of the serial.

Stan's acting was negligible to the point of invisibility. He seldom had a solo camera shot, and aside from singing, had few lines to deliver. He was mainly used as a sounding board for the other adult actors. Stan's manner was soft-spoken and gentlemanly. He was never seen without a book or his guitar and was well-liked by the folks at Disney.

Stan's charity work included an assignment to promote the President's Committee on Employment of the Physically Handicapped. Musicians would donate their talent to the *America Sings* project, a "program of folk songs of our land" that was presented as radio broadcasts combining musical entertainment and public service announcements. Stan, backing himself on guitar, begins the show with a stripped down, abbreviated version of "Ghost Riders." He breaks off after the first verse and a round of "yipi-yi-ays" and "yipi-yi-os" to declare the good cause he's there to encourage—that all American employers should consider hiring the handicapped. He then performs an old folk tune, "Noah's Dove," a rare instance in which he sings a song he hadn't written. He continues with a strong rendition of "Cottonwood Tree," one of the handful of songs he had recorded on *Creakin' Leather*, with just his guitar. After another public service pitch, Stan implores, "Mr. Employer, check your plant for job openings. This is Stan Jones saying, it's good business to hire the handicapped." He introduces his next song, "Cowpoke," about "a real cowboy, not the Hollywood variety," and then launches into the overlooked gem he had written back in Death Valley.

The lyrics of "Cowpoke," inspired by Stan's memories of the old-time cowboys encountered during his Douglas days, celebrate the glad buckaroos who cling to a solitary, near-impoverished lifestyle, choosing to live under the stars, accompanied only by a good horse, and ranging within spitting distance of a herd of bawling cattle: "I'm lonesome but happy / I'm rich but I'm broke / And the good lord knows the reason / I'm just a cowpoke / From Cheyenne down to Douglas / All the ranges I know / 'Cause I drift with the wind / No one cares where I go." Burdened by layers of echoing background vocals amid a jaunty banjo-driven musical arrangement, Stan's first recorded version of "Cowpoke" on *This Was The West* failed to capture the spare elegance of this first-rate song. In his unadorned guitar and voice rendition on the *America Sings* program, Stan's casual, animated style compellingly conveys a freewheeling western character whose career choice has made him a "carefree, range ridin', driftin' Cowpoke."

Finally, Stan introduced his last selection on the program:

> Well sir, I've been a miner, a logger, a ranger, cowpuncher, sailor . . . and
> I've sung an awful lot of songs in a lot of places on this earth, but of all of
> 'em that I've ever heard or sung, this is my favorite: "The Burro Lullaby."

He tenderly crooned his languorous ode of love to Olive and Death Valley, made one final pitch for hiring the handicapped, and then signed off: "This is Stan Jones from my ranch in Douglas, Arizona, saying, thanks for listening."

Stan's most memorable compositions exhibit his clever talent for slipping in clues that alluded to his deeply held spiritual beliefs and the occasional nod to his own Arizona heritage. In "Cowpoke," he deliberately chose to honor his roots with the lines "From Cheyenne down to Douglas / All the ranges I know," when he just as easily could have used the name of a town that carried a bit more melodramatic heft such as Tombstone or even Tucson. The "Cowpoke" verse that exclaims "I can pick up a ten spot / In Prescott I know" pays tribute to another historic Arizona town, albeit one that carried a sadder connotation for Stan as the resting place of the father he never knew. After Stan had artfully inserted a reference to "Ghost Riders" in his great cowboy gospel song, "Saddle Up," the verse that follows proclaims triumphantly, "You never really ever died / So saddle up and ride!"

CHAPTER 17

YOU NEVER REALLY
EVER DIED

STAN WAS INVOLVED WITH A NEW RECORDING PROJECT, ANNOUNCED by Hedda Hopper on January 6, 1961, the last time she would mention Stan in her gossip column before his death. She announced: "That lovable Walter Brennan has already made three albums, is about to do a fourth with songs by Stan Jones, who used to compose for Disney and did 'Ghost Riders in the Sky.'"

Producer-arranger Joe Leahy's newly formed label, Record Producer's Corporation, was set to debut a series of three albums utilizing "the nostalgic approach in their material, spotlighting the 'good old days' theme performed by established movie and TV names." Dick Powell narrated *The Teen Years*, Loretta Young was the chosen vocal lead for *Remembered Years*, and Walter Brennan was the star for his collaboration with Stan, which was titled *By The Fireside*.

Referred to by Stan in the liner notes for the album as "this tall, sweet, dour, gently rough, thoroughly honest replica of Uncle Sam himself," Brennan enjoyed a huge wave of popularity from the ABC television show *The Real McCoys*. Introduced for the first time at a dinner party in late 1960, Stan and "Grandpa McCoy" hit it off immediately. The concept was hatched for the narrative and musical framework of *By The Fireside* after a subsequent meeting in Stan's den, when the two men, facing a crackling blaze in the big stone fireplace, shared their respective visions of western history and how the

Courtesy of the author

frontier experience played a role in shaping modern America. Stan expounds
in the liner notes:

> Mr. Brennan takes you on a mythical, yet very real journey of a real
> American's life, from way down East on the coast of Massachusetts as a
> young boy, to the placid and reverent content of the San Fernando Valley
> as a modern-day grandfather. He does this surrounded by all his family and
> close friends, from his comfortable big chair, and he does it exactly as you
> would expect him to . . . transporting you into the depths of real Ameri-
> cana, typifying the typical American family, in narration, song, and poetry,
> all in "Brennanese," so loved by us all.

"Brennanese" refers to the distinctive "Amos McCoy" vocal shtick employed
by Brennan while playing the cantankerous old grandpa on the television

show that was regularly viewed by as many as fifty million Americans weekly. Walter Brennan recites Stan's narrative as his fictional family, consisting of his son, daughter-in-law, and grandchildren, gathered around a crackling fire in a 1960s-era family room, listen on. The story of the restless search for happiness and inner peace by Brennan's character often mirrors the "mythical, yet very real journey" of Stan's life. The wayfarer's episodic travels are accentuated by Stan's musical compositions. Encompassing a migration across a swath of the continental United States, Stan's protagonist is reared on the East Coast and then migrates to the Great Plains. He eventually wanders farther west to a cattle ranch in Colorado, and finally lands in suburban Los Angeles, nestled in the bosom of his beloved family.

Stan created two discontented, edgy souls, who are met along the way by the young wanderer, who share their profound regrets about not settling down to hearth and home when they were younger. The "old first mate" may very well be based on a veteran sailor whom Stan had met during his apprentice seaman's days in the navy. The old salt explains to the "sapling" that after forty years of seafaring he's staying on shore for good to give himself a shot at settling down with the woman he loves. He urges the young man, "Don't ever try and find somethin' somewheres else that was always right there in your heart to begin with." This wistful counsel leads into "Deep Water," Stan's song first recorded for *Creakin' Leather,* that contains the line, "You can never really leave home."

The theme from *The Searchers* is then resurrected to amplify the longings of "the old cowpuncher," a personage probably modeled on Stan's boyhood hero, Capp Watts. Blubbering that "he'd waited too long" to settle down, the creaky old cuss is forced to leave the cowpoke life behind him for good and "ride away" on the very day that Stan's alter-ego arrives at the Colorado ranch. These circumspect tales of woe echo the cautionary message offered by Stan in "Ghost Riders" as "Cowboy change your ways today or with us you will ride." In Stan's vision, you can choose between a path leading to inner spiritual peace, or you can damn well suit yourself and be doomed to an eternity of "A-try'n to catch the devil's herd / across these endless skies."

Stan's vagabond gets the message, finds a gal to hitch his wagon to, and we are then transported back around the family fire as the daughter-in-law asks, "What's the happiest thing that has ever happened to you, Amos?" Ol' Grandpa responds with, "Well sir, I turned into something like a shiny new fence post!" when given the news that his first son had been born. For this event in the story, Stan was doubtlessly reflecting on the blessed arrival of his new son, Stan Jr. The proud and grateful father wrote a lullaby-style prayer, titled "Little Son," with the final lines, reverently intoned by the studio choir: "For in my heart I'll love always, for this, my little son / Amen."

Grandpa caps off the evening by sharing the cumulative moral of Stan's allegorical tale, that if you pay attention to what your heart tells you, real peace is best garnered from within. In his final song written for the album, "Peace Within," Stan couldn't resist adding the caveat that, in his experience, the great outdoors is ultimately more conducive to gaining inner peace than the urban environs of the San Fernando Valley: "Out where the sidewalks are no more / Where bright lights have never been / There is a mountain and valley / There is peace within."

Stan was undoubtedly envisioning Mount Rainier and Death Valley as the "mountain and valley" where inner satisfaction was most easily attained. The gist of the storyline contained in *By The Fireside* parallels the oftentimes crooked pathway Stan trudged along in his own personal journey before finding his feet by settling down with Olive. Even though he resided in the heart of the Los Angeles basin, Stan Jones had discovered his own personal brand of "peace within."

The album, *By The Fireside,* failed to make a dent in the *Billboard* charts and remains an obscure relic from a distant age of American culture. When heard today it's hard to imagine a loftier pinnacle of early 1960s camp than that achieved by Walter Brennan "rapping" Stan's lyrics in Amos McCoy vernacular over a cornball banjo and harmonica arrangement of the "The Lilies Grow High." What can finally be gleaned from Stan's effort in *By The Fireside* is his unabashed sincerity and adamant drive to tell and retell the story of the American experience filtered through the singular vision born of his own personal odyssey, fused with the frontier ghosts from a past epoch that he stubbornly continued to harbor in his mind's eye.

Stan made one last stab at realizing his dream of filming a feature-length movie in Douglas and recruited Andrew Brennan, son of Walter, to be an associate producer of the project. Under the headline "Riders in the Sky Picture To Be Made At John Slaughter Ranch," the August 6, 1962, *Douglas Daily Dispatch* reported that Stan was in town to make the arrangements for the production to be shot on location at the Slaughter ranch come February

Stan's final promotional portrait, 1962. *Photofest. Used by permission.*

"if present planning is followed." Stan reported, "included in the cast will be the cavalry, Indians and cowpokes, and local people will be used as much as possible," and that he wanted "*Riders in the Sky* produced here because this is where he first heard the story."

His intention was to, naturally, weave "the old cowpuncher" Capp Watts into the screenplay. Stan awarded him two fictional sons in the script, perhaps to make amends for the phantom family that Capp was too old to foster in *By The Fireside*. Stan also allowed that a few interior scenes of *Riders in the Sky* would likely be shot in the St. Stephen's Episcopal Church. He left town a few days later with high hopes, but as was often the norm with Hollywood projects in development, "present planning" failed to pan out. Not long after, the onetime rather ordinary local boy who ended up writing one extraordinary song would return one final time to Douglas.

For many years, Stan mysteriously held to the belief that he was living on borrowed time. According to Dobe Carey, "Stan always said he was going to die when he was in his forties. I don't know what made him get that planted in his head, but he always said, 'I won't be around by then, I'll be gone.' It was a very strange thing."

The premonition Stan revealed to Carey held true. In the fall of 1963, Lloyd Perryman, one of Stan and Olive's closest friends, became aware that Stan had developed cancer. An operation in August to remove a lung to staunch the spread of the disease proved to be futile. Perryman recalled his final visit with Stan:

> He was deteriorating and it was a pretty sad sight because Stan was such an active man, very quick in his actions. The last time I saw him it was kind of a heartbreaking thing because he was lying on the sofa in his home. It was obvious to me that Stan was aware that this was about it.

Stan Jones died at the age of forty-nine on Friday, December 13, 1963, at the Queen of Angels Hospital in Los Angeles. He was buried on December 17 at Calvary Memorial Park in Douglas, Arizona.

Stan hadn't shared his condition beyond a small nucleus of family and friends. Johnny Western could not believe that the Singing Ranger was dead:

> Sure, Stan was a chain smoker, but I was stunned, you know, forty-nine years old and he just dropped like a rock. He was there one day and he wasn't the next. Dobe or Ben or nobody knew. Stan never said anything to me. He was this feisty little guy and I didn't think you could kill him with an ax. When I got the news that Stan had died I thought, he's just a young guy, he was older than me, but late forties is way, way, way too young to die.

Venerable Los Angeles newscaster George Putnam (no relation to George Palmer Putnam of Stovepipe Wells) had known Stan since the early 1950s when he read advertisements on the Sons of the Pioneers' *Lucky U Ranch* radio show. Putnam took the exceptional step of reserving a few minutes during his Monday evening newscast to read a tribute to Stan. Written by the Joneses' good friend, author and television screenwriter Turnley Walker, Stan was praised for both his humane and creative strengths: "In his songs and other writing and in himself, he gave all he had to give . . . and he will always live because the things he loved and had the talent to express must always stay alive in us." He wrote of the enduring twinkle in Stan's eyes and how it sparkled until the very end:

> A man who gave gentleness and compassion and relief from spiritual pain to every life he touched . . . died last Friday evening after suffering without complaint the agonies of an idiot malevolence called cancer. He died bravely . . . which meant that in his last few conscious moments he managed a little of his wry humor to relieve the suffering of those who loved him and were there.

The graveside services in Douglas, arranged by George Rogers, were held on a Tuesday afternoon and were officiated by the rector of the St. Stephen's Episcopal Church, the Reverend J. G. J. van Moort, whom Stan had met with the previous summer while trying to arrange the production schedule for his movie. Stan's physician and long time friend from Hollywood, Dr. Henry J. Lange, accompanied Olive to the services and read a poem that Stan had written in 1950 titled "Resurrectus." The final stanza is cast onto the rectangular brass plaque that marks his gravesite:

> I'll see Him in the sunrise
> Or just as day is done
> No more to walk in darkness
> For I know now—
> My cares are none.

In a typed letter to Stan's mother Berta, dated January 1, 1964, Stan and Olive's twentieth wedding anniversary, Olive wrote:

> Dearest Granny,
>
> I have wanted to write sooner, but some how or other just couldn't.
>
> I know you want to know about the graveside ceremony in Douglas. It was beautiful. Dr. Lange read "Resurrectus" and then the Dutch minister gave a simple service.

The afternoon was warm and sunny; not even a breeze stirred. It could be described as great tranquility. There were many people there, perhaps 50 or even a hundred, and although flowers were not requested, there were thirteen lovely sprays from people in Douglas beside the beautiful casket spray from friends in Nevada.

Several friends chartered planes and flew in from Phoenix. All in all, you would have been very pleased. The little cemetery is perpetually cared for, with lawn and little cypresses on it. The plot for Stan had a little pine tree on it. I know how hard this has been for you. Stan loved you very much.

As for me, there is an emptiness that can never be replaced. But I feel blessed and am grateful that I had twenty years with Stan and that I have his precious little son. Stan is really very close to all of us. God bless you.

After signing her name in longhand, Olive wrote on the back of the letter the names of Stan's pallbearers who Berta may have recognized. After the name of Percy Bowden, she added in parentheses, "Stan used to mow his lawn," and following the name of Phil Olander, Olive noted: "Sheriff of Cochise."

Johnny Western remained confounded that his friend and songwriting mentor was suddenly gone. He and country singer Jerry Inman had traveled from Los Angeles to play a handful of shows in southern Arizona a few months after Stan's death and found themselves in Douglas on the last weekend of March 1964. After a few inquiries following Saturday night's performance, Johnny learned the location of the local cemetery and he and Inman paid a visit to Stan's grave the following morning, Easter Sunday. Johnny remembered, "It was really windy that morning, very windy, and people had already been out early on Sunday morning after mass or whatever church they went to and put Easter lilies on the graves." Western had recorded "The Lilies Grow High" in 1962 and was telling Jerry Inman how much Stan and his music had meant to him:

> We were standing at the foot of the grave and I was talking to Jerry about "The Lilies Grow High." I was looking out over Stan's grave and I said, "Stan, if you're up there, and you can hear me, and you know that I'm standing here at the foot of your grave, looking at the Cochise Stronghold from right here, I wish to hell you'd give me a sign to let me know you

are listening" . . . and I swear on a stack of Bibles, and Jerry can back me up the whole way, I'd no sooner finished saying that when a gust of wind came up, and down this little dusty path came a bundle of Easter lilies that somebody had put on a grave. The wind had picked them up and rolled them and rolled them and they were making little dust devils as the wind was blowing them toward us. They had a band around them so they held together, and they landed right at my feet.

The hair stood up on the back of my neck and Jerry's eyes got as big as saucers and I said, "Oh my God Jerry, do you know what just happened?" He couldn't even talk, he was just frozen. I just know to this day that Stan heard me and that was the sign I was asking for. That was my final encounter with Stan Jones.

On Christmas eve day 1963, Olive was attending to the loose ends of Stan's affairs and sent off a copy of his Standard School Broadcast album, *I Am An American,* and the following letter to the Jones's good friend in Phoenix, Allen Reed:

Dear Allen—

Enclosed is the album that Stan had planned to autograph for your Christmas. It was the last work he completed before his illness, when he had a lung removed in August.

His determination and faith to win the battle was so strong that it was unbelievable when he passed away Dec. 13th. The odds were against him.

Ultimately, the odds are mercilessly weighed against all of us. Olive's dear husband, Stan Jones, had a leg up on immortality though—he had written one immortal song.

CHAPTER 18

GHOST RIDERS IN THE SKY

A VIDEO CLIP IN MARTIN SCORSESE'S 2011 DOCUMENTARY ABOUT George Harrison, *Living in the Material World*, features four musicians jammed around a kitchen table strumming guitars and singing the chorus to "Ghost Riders in the Sky." Jeff Lynne, Tom Petty, George Harrison, and Bob Dylan (known collectively with Roy Orbison as the Traveling Wilburys) are belting out "Yipi-yi-ay . . . Yipi-yi-o . . . Ghost Riders in the Sky"—an instantly recognizable melody to music lovers around the world.

Search any Internet music download site and you'll find hundreds of recorded versions of "Ghost Riders in the Sky" in just about every musical genre imaginable. Contemporary recordings include an exquisite version by Judy Collins on her 2010 album, *Paradise*. The Broadway musical, *Million Dollar Quartet*, chronicles the day in 1956 that Johnny Cash, Elvis Presley, Carl Perkins, and Jerry Lee Lewis gathered for an impromptu jam session at Sun Studios in Memphis. A solid rendering of "Ghost Riders" is performed by the actor who portrays Johnny Cash, even though it was not on the roster of tunes sung at the fabled 1956 gathering. Folk artist Mary McCaslin has recorded a graceful acoustic reading of Stan's song that stands out for its spare beauty and elegance. The San Francisco Gay Men's Chorus recorded a brawny a cappella version. Children of Bodom, Finland's favorite death metal band, recorded a requisitely gloomy interpretation of Stan's cowboy ballad.

The 2007 film, *Ghost Rider*, based on a Marvel Comics character, features a great rock and roll version of "Ghost Riders in the Sky" performed by the Australian alt-rock band, Spiderbait. As of this writing there are more than seven million hits on the YouTube videos that combine scenes from the film and Spiderbait's recording of "Ghost Riders." Instrumental covers of "Jinetes En El Cielo" (Riders in the Sky) by Latin American bands remain in demand south of the border.

Folk musicians in Germany regularly perform "Geisterreiter" at festivals celebrating the American West. On the vast Tohono O'odham reservation in Southern Arizona, Native American instrumental bands perform dance music stemming from Mexican polka traditions called waila and "Ghost Riders" is one of their most popular songs. Riders in the Sky, the gifted band that sustains the western music tradition of the Sons of the Pioneers, has performed more than six thousand shows worldwide since 1977, and at each and every one "the song that named the band" retains a hallowed place on their set list. "Ghost Riders in the Sky" remains deeply infused throughout myriad American musical traditions. Barring a cataclysmic collapse of western civilization, it's here to stay.

"Ghost Riders in the Sky" holds a well-deserved place in the pantheon of legendary American songs. What is it that makes it such an extraordinary and unforgettable composition? In his 1949 foreword, written to accompany the sheet music of "Riders in the Sky: A Cowboy Legend," Burl Ives concisely sums up the song's twin strengths: "It has rich imagery in its language, and it has music of imagination and integrity." "Ghost Riders" touched a chord deep within a populace that had witnessed half a century of global wars, economic depression, and watershed advancements in the arts and sciences. Stan's "rich imagery" transported listeners to a realm not normally explored in popular music.

The blurry-eyed, sweat-stained cowboys gallop relentlessly after the devil's herd up in the mythical terrain of the heavens, where gods and goddesses have fought, loved, and soared in ancient stories told since the dawn of human consciousness. Here was a parable in song, employing contemporary western themes that captured adult listeners' imaginations in a way that fairy tales entrance children, drawing them into a vivid story told with bold, cinematic images to impart a durable life lesson: "Cowboy change your ways today or with us you will ride / A-tryin' to catch the devil's herd / Across these endless skies." The haunting, "mournful cry" echoes of the "Yipi-yi-ay,

Yipi-yi-o" chorus seal the deal. This was a song unlike any other written or recorded in the twentieth century.

Not only are the lyrics to "Ghost Riders" captivating, the tensile strength of the clear, declarative melody enhances the overall power of the story. By shifting the foundation of the melody line back and forth from the vaguely ominous resonance of a minor chord to the brighter voicing of a major chord, Stan's music attains the aural equivalent of a thunderstorm, blending light and dark tonalities that evoke the dramatic, unsettled skies where the lyrical action unfolds. Of the countless number of recordings made of "Ghost Riders" over the past decades, it's noteworthy that roughly a third are instrumentals, testimony to the fact that the musical theme of "Ghost Riders" has the inherent melodic strength to stand on its own. To use plain language, "Ghost Riders in the Sky" is simply a great song, no matter how you cut it.

Speculation on the origins of the "cowboy legend" that Capp Watts passed on to Stan usually revolves around two sources: an ancient European myth dubbed "The Wild Hunt" and the "Legend of Stampede Mesa," a Texas folk tale that was told around cowboy campfires in the Southwest during the latter part of the nineteenth century. The possibility that Capp was familiar with one or both of these is likely. The surname Watts has Germanic roots and some story form of "The Wild Hunt" myth might have been passed down through the generations to Capp. The gist of the grim scenario features "a phantasmal leader, accompanied by a horde of hounds and men, hurdling through the night sky, their passing marked by a tumultuous racket of pounding hooves, howling dogs, and raging winds." A variation from the Orkney Islands tells of ghostly maidens out on midnight rides, "galloping furiously through the air," who were often seen "driving a stolen cow before them."

The "Wild Hunt" myth invariably threads two constant themes together: the action always proceeds through a violent thunderstorm, and those who witness the ghastly procession face certain disaster or death. Stan Jones never told his version of how he was introduced to the "Ghost Riders" the same way twice. In June of 1949, RCA produced a promotional recording to inform disc jockeys and their national record distributors of "the story behind the song" that suggests evidence to link "Riders in the Sky" directly to "The

Wild Hunt" legend. Vaughn Monroe himself recited this interpretation, which he claims at the beginning of the recording was "told a friend of mine by Stan Jones":

> The legend declares that the ghost herd can only be seen on cloudy, gloomy days and anyone who sees the "Riders in the Sky" is doomed. Many ranch hands, including Stan, scoffed at the idea of this visual premonition of death until one day—a dark, dreary day when Stan, in his early teens, was out on his father's range, alone mending fences. While riding over the desolate prairie, he suddenly noticed a friend of his, an old cowhand, sitting still as a statue on his horse atop a mesa on a high plateau, staring at the sky. Stan helloed to his friend—no response. Then he yelled and waved, but still no response. He raced to the spot, but the old cowboy didn't turn until Stan was right beside him. He didn't say hello. Huddled in his poncho, he turned quietly and said, "I just saw the Riders in the Sky. I'm going to die." And with that the cowhand rode away.
>
> When Stan returned home he told the story to his father, who shrugged it away as a silly superstition, not worth another thought. The next morning, Stan's friend did not turn up for breakfast. They went looking for him—found him in his bunk, dead.

A fabled clash between a cattleman named Sawyer and a homesteader (derisively called "nesters" by established ranchers) in Crosby County, Texas, in the 1880s, underlies the "Legend of Stampede Mesa." A small herd of the nester's cattle had mixed in with the cattleman's and the whole bunch ended up on a high, peninsular mesa surrounded on three sides by steep bluffs. Sawyer ignored the nester's pleas to cut his cows away from the main herd. That night the nester sneaked up onto the mesa and blasted a shot from his pistol that stampeded hundreds of steers over the cliffs to their deaths, taking two of Sawyer's cowboys with them. The following day Sawyer's remaining men captured the nester, strapped him onto his blindfolded horse, and backed him off the mesa's edge to smash amid the cattle carcasses at the base of the bluff. The story's told: "Old cowpunchers say that if you chance to be about Stampede Mesa at night, you can hear the nester calling his cattle, and many assert that they have seen his murdered ghost, astride a blindfolded horse, sweeping over the headlands, behind a stampeding herd of phantom steers."

A blacksmith for a big cattle outfit in Kingsville, Texas, around the turn of the twentieth century recalled cowboys arriving back from long spells on the range declaring, "Well, I saw the ghost herd while night herdin' and I guess I either give up drinkin' and bad ways or I'm not goin' to be around long." Evidence that Stan himself believed that a glimpse of the "phantom steers" portended certain death is on a note scribbled to his nephew Bill Dubs on the 1949 sheet music of Burl Ives's "Riders in the Sky": "To William—The little nephew I used to 'practice' on 15 years ago[1]—Good luck buck and may you never see the herd. —Stan"

It may never be ascertained where exactly Capp Watts drew the inspiration for his particular vision of the Ghost Riders. Perhaps a morphing of the "Wild Hunt" and the "Stampede Mesa" legends reached Capp somewhere in his travels from Texas to Arizona as the version that he eventually passed on to young Stan Jones, perhaps not. Regardless of how and where the legend was born, Stan's adolescent experience with Capp under the menacing skies east of Douglas branded a palpable, frightening vision into his fragile young imagination.

Part of the genius of his rendering the Ghost Riders' saga into song lies in the keen poetry of the lyrics. Stan places us up on that ridge and forces us to see those "black and shiny" horns of the "red-eyed cows." We shudder at the arrival of the riders "on horses snortin' fire" and "comin' hard" out of the stormy darkness as they wail their "mournful cry." And when the riders call our name and offer the recourse to "save your soul from hell a-ridin' on our range," there's no argument. By the end of this nightmare journey, we are shaken but relieved witnesses of Stan's celestial parable. We stand gratefully, with feet planted on the solid earth, gazing after the doomed ghosts as they gallop and fade into the "endless skies."

The semblance between the opening lines of "Ghost Riders in the Sky" and "When Johnny Comes Marching Home" has been bandied about in the press and numerous other accounts of Stan's song since the original comparative reference was made in the May 2, 1949, issue of *Time* magazine: "The first publisher who heard Riders told him [Stan] it sounded too much like a 'funeral dirge or a college hymn.' (Actually, its opening sounded more like the first few steps of When Johnny Comes Marching Home.)"

---

[1] According to Bill Dubs this reference to "practicing" relates to his Uncle Stan's playing the guitar for him sometime during 1934.

Besides being "too wordy," the Sons of the Pioneers reportedly passed on "Ghost Riders" as also "too derivative" of "When Johnny Comes Marching Home," when they had a crack at recording it before Vaughn Monroe in 1949. Spend a little time either humming or singing the opening lines to both songs back-to-back and you might catch a relationship between the two. "Johnny's" sharp staccato rhythm that snaps in with the words "When Johnny comes marching home again, Hoorah! Hoorah!" lacks the loping grace of, "An old cowpoke went ridin' out one dark and windy day." Still, if you kick the lines around long enough, it is possible to acknowledge a resemblance between them.

Stan Jones steadfastly believed he had indeed "borrowed" from the old Civil War ballad. Johnny Western recalls how he and Stan "cemented their friendship" over the issue. Western was barely out of his teens when he moved to Los Angeles to pursue an acting career as a "Singing Cowboy" in 1955. In his home state of Minnesota at the age of five, his fate had been sealed after seeing the Gene Autry western, *Guns and Guitars.* He was fourteen when he first heard Vaughn Monroe's "Ghost Riders in the Sky" on the radio. Plowing nickel after nickel into an ice cream shop jukebox, Johnny copied down the words, learned the chords, and sang "Ghost Riders" on his first local radio performance a short time thereafter, launching a long, successful career as a musician, television actor, and radio personality.

He met Stan at a 1956 New Year's party, and Western couldn't believe his good fortune at befriending the man who had written "the most popular song in western music." He began to play bit parts in the many television westerns that were being produced in and around Los Angeles at the time. After playing a role on *Have Gun Will Travel,* he became inspired to write a song for the star of the show, Richard Boone, as a thank you for the opportunity to work with him. On the day that he was pacing the floor in March of 1958, awaiting news of the birth of his second child, "Ghost Riders in the Sky" kept running through Johnny's head. He picked up his guitar and a legal pad and wrote "The Ballad of Paladin" in about twenty minutes. A few days later he delivered a demo to Richard Boone and before long he signed a contract with CBS to record his song that became the end theme for *Have Gun Will Travel.* The novice songwriter guiltily called up his buddy Stan:

"Stan, I think I owe you something big time." He said, "What?" I said, "Well, I stole part of 'Ghost Riders' for this new TV theme song I'm doing for CBS." And he said, "Well, what did you steal?" I said, "The beat." "The beat?" "Yeah," I said. "You know, ta da da da ta da da da . . ." He started laughing hysterically. He had that Stan Jones laugh—when you hit the punch line of a joke he would just fall down laughing with tears in his eyes. He was laughing all over the house, I could tell he was walking with the telephone. I asked, "What's the matter?" He said, "You can't copyright a beat—anybody can use that beat, and besides all songwriters steal. I stole 'Ghost Riders.'" I said, "You've got to be kidding! Stan, 'Ghost Riders' is the most unique song that I've heard in my entire life!" He said, "You think so?" I said, "I know so." He said, "Sing me the first line of 'Ghost Riders.'" I sang, "An old cowpoke went riding out one dark and windy day." He sang, "When Johnny comes marching home again, hurrah hurrah."

Music publisher Edwin "Buddy" Morris added "Ghost Riders" to his impressive array of finely crafted popular tunes in 1949. When Morris was inducted into the Songwriters Hall of Fame in 1994, the official tribute to his career heralded the roster of master songwriters and songs that he had assembled for his publishing company in the 1940s. The tribute singled out a few of the most memorable compositions associated with Edwin H. Morris & Company:

> The songs these writers turned out for Edwin H. Morris added up to a veritable hit parade of the era. They included "Autumn Leaves," "Tenderly," "Sentimental Journey," "Ghost Riders in the Sky," "The Christmas Song," "The Man That Got Away," "Witchcraft," and "Route 66."

The list of composers associated with Morris included Ira Gershwin, Sammy Cahn, Jimmy Van Huesen, Harold Arlen, and Johnny Mercer—august company for a spindly little cowpoke from Cochise County.

When Morris's company[2] published the sheet music in 1949, it was with the title, "Riders in the Sky (A Cowboy Legend)." Why the word "ghost" was not originally included is a mystery. It slowly weaved its way into the primary title over the years, although "ghost" is sometimes presented in parentheses, as in Johnny Cash's 1979 recording "(Ghost) Riders in the Sky." "A Cowboy

[2] Paul McCartney purchased Edwin H. Morris & Company in 1976 and, via his MPL Communications Corporation, owns the publishing rights to "Ghost Riders in the Sky."

Legend" was included in the title of Vaughn Monroe's original release but has been rarely used since 1949. Stan wrote the first chorus as "ghost herd in the sky" to reflect the beginning verse where the "old cowpoke" first spots the cloud-borne cattle. Thereafter, once the "riders" have entered the scene, the chorus becomes "Ghost Riders in the Sky." Stan intended the final chorus line to be repeated twice, the first using "ghost herd in the sky" and then finally "Ghost Riders in the Sky." The "Yipi-yi-ays" and "Yipi-yi-os" were transcribed to be repeated in that respective order. Burl Ives, in his premier recording of Stan's song, faithfully tracked the sheet music verbatim. Vaughn Monroe slipped in two "yipi-yi-os" in one chorus and at the end of the final chorus uses only the "Ghost Riders in the Sky" line. The artists who covered "Ghost Riders" throughout the 1950s generally modeled their interpretations on the classic vocal and instrumental arrangement spawned by Charles Grean and Vaughn Monroe.

A trend to record the song sans vocals was initiated in the early 1960s by The Ramrods, an instrumental rock and roll group hailing from the East Coast. Influenced by the twangy, reverb-heavy guitar styling of Duane Eddy, they recorded "Ghost Riders" in December of 1960, complete with cattle-drive sound effects of hoots, whistles, and bawling cows. The Ramrods version of Stan's song fared well on the pop charts, rising to number thirty in February of 1961, spurring other "surf guitar" artists, such as the Ventures and Dick Dale, to throw their cowboy hats into the ring. European instrumental bands the Scorpions, from England, and a Swedish group, the Spotnicks, were inspired by The Ramrod's take on "Ghost Riders" and recorded their versions of the famous American song in 1961. Hundreds of instrumental recordings of "Ghost Riders" have ensued during the past fifty years in genres ranging from "pops" orchestras to jazz to bluegrass. Instrumental breaks in vocal versions of "Ghost Riders" are almost exclusively a repeat of the melody line with little variation on the primary musical theme.

Johnny Cash chose to record "Ghost Riders" in 1979 and his version sounds as if Stan Jones wrote "Ghost Riders in the Sky" just so Cash could sing it. Fused with an innovative arrangement featuring heraldic horns, articulate piano accents, and a subtle background female vocal choir shading the chorus, the magisterial authority of Cash's vocal delivery elevated Stan's song to new dramatic heights. Olive Jones didn't see it that way though. Johnny Western recalled, "Olive hated his version when it came out because he [Cash] had changed the words to 'an old cowboy' instead of 'cowpoke' and sang the 'Yipi-yi-ay, Yipi-yi-o' chorus backwards. When the huge royalty checks started rolling in, she changed her mind about that."

Stan's great nephew, Keeter Stuart, shed the Fanner 50s of his gunslingin' youth for a guitar to become an accomplished musical ambassador for his Uncle Stan's extensive song catalogue. His CD *Ghost Riders, Searchers, & Cowpokes: The Timeless Songs of Stan Jones*, recorded in 2008, is an exceptional introduction to many of Stan's fine compositions that have languished in the shadow of "Ghost Riders." A highlight of the collection finds Stuart harmonizing in the studio with his Uncle Stan's original recording of "Burro Lullaby," drawn from Stan's first Disney album *Creakin' Leather*. Finely wrought renditions of "Cowpoke," "The Searchers," and "The Lilies Grow High" exemplify the depth and quality of Stan Jones's reach as a creative artist. A remarkably fresh take on "Ghost Riders" is included, driven by an intriguing Caribbean rhythmic feel, and sporting a tasteful lead break played on a tiple, a small, five-stringed Latin American instrument. *Ghost Riders, Searchers, & Cowpokes* is the perfect "one-stop-shop" to gain an appreciation for the range of first-rate songs that Stan composed throughout his career.

Stuart's first recorded version of "Ghost Riders in the Sky," found on his debut CD titled *Just*, is a fabulously rollicking, honky-tonk rush. Full of Fender guitar twang smartly integrated with flute and tenor saxophone highlights, Stuart and his band hit inspirational heights on this cut rarely achieved on any studio-produced song. He attributed the magic feel of the session to a host of "visitors":

> I was recording my first CD at my buddy's house in Oregon. We knew we were going to be recording a couple of Uncle Stan's songs, so I brought over an old publicity photo of Stan, which we propped on a stool in the corner of the studio, lit by a couple of votive candles. We were hoping that ol' Stan's spirit might look kindly on our efforts. That evening, we were running through "Ghost Riders." We were on the fourth or fifth take, things were really getting good, the song was peaking . . . The lights in the studio dimmed suddenly, followed immediately by a tremendous clap of thunder. We stopped playing and stood for a moment in stunned silence. There was no storm coming, no forecast of rain—what was going on?
>
> We ran outside to see. There were no clouds overhead, but when we looked to the south, we saw a dark, roiling squall of clouds about a mile away passing along the ridgeline. There was a pale moon above, but no

other clouds in sight. Suddenly, the lightning flashed inside the squall and the thunder roared toward us again. It felt like a good omen . . . the hairs on the back of my neck were standing up and tingling. We all had the same thought as we looked at each other; it's them! It's the Ghost Riders!

What a night, what a song, what a wonderful, magical mystery that was. . . . Ride on Stan, and thanks.

Stan understood that he had sealed his destiny on the front porch of the Emigrant Ranger Station many years past. The song he composed on that quiet Sunday morning blazed out of him like a lightning bolt flashing over the Arizona desert. The drama of Capp Watts's celestial riders chasing that herd of cows across the clouds had remained lodged in his imagination for more than twenty years. Stan's revelation, grounded in his religious beliefs and life experience, that choices have consequences, stirred him to fashion "Ghost Riders in the Sky" as a cautionary tale: the gaunt, sweaty cowboys doomed to gallop after those steel-hooved steers for all eternity were up there for a reason. It's not important to nail down the exact date that he composed "Ghost Riders in the Sky," or to say for sure whether on that particular Sunday morning there were storm clouds hanging over the ranger station that ignited his inner muse: what we do know for certain is that one morning in Death Valley, Stan Jones created a song for the ages.

How sublimely perfect that "Ghost Riders in the Sky," a haunting revelation of cowboy purgatory, was written in the ethereal vastness of Death Valley, the desert wilderness that Olive learned to embrace alongside her husband. And how truly fitting that Stan lies at rest under the borderland skies of Douglas where the inspiration for one of the most renowned songs in the annals of popular music was born. As long as there is a guitar and an American songbook on this earth, the legacy of the gifted, big-hearted Arizonan, Stan Jones, will live on. You never really ever died, Stan; you knew in your heart all along you were destined to saddle up and ride, forever and ever, across those endless skies.

EPILOGUE

STAN JONES WAS POSTHUMOUSLY INDUCTED INTO THE WESTERN MUSIC Association Hall of Fame in 1997. Representatives from the Association traveled to Tarzana to award the official plaque to Olive Jones and Stan Jones Jr., the son that she and Stan had together in 1960, known to the family as SJ. An informal ceremony was held at the house on Casa Drive, where photos were taken of Olive, SJ, and one of his two young sons, Nathan, all with big smiles arm-in-arm on the brick patio. Olive had not returned to Death Valley since she and Stan had last visited the Pipkins at Wildrose in the early 1950s, and her family decided it was time to pay a visit to the place where "Ghost Riders in the Sky" had been written.

The day arrived for the Jones clan to venture out to the desert and a last-minute reservation was made to accommodate them at the Furnace Creek Ranch that evening. Olive and Stan Jr., along with his wife and two sons, climbed into a van and drove the three hundred miles northeast of Los Angeles toward Death Valley National Park. They entered the park from the Panamint Valley via Wildrose, where Olive pointed out the site in the narrow canyon where George and Ann Pipkin's small resort operation once stood. A mile further up the road they took a short detour at the turnoff to the Charcoal Kilns that led to the site of the old summer headquarters where Stan and a disheartened Olive arrived in the dead of night in August 1946. All that remained from the days of shifting the park operations from Cow Creek to Wildrose for the summer were three wooden cabins and a large, weathered, tin-sided garage.

By early evening, without much daylight to spare, SJ guided the van into the parking area across from the old stone ranger station at Emigrant. The building had been vacant since the late 1980s, and except for the addition of a pay phone at the southeast corner of the front porch, it looked exactly as it had appeared to Stan and Olive when they first saw it more than fifty years before. The deadline for arriving at the Ranch to claim their rooms was looming. It was a forty-minute drive from Emigrant to Furnace Creek and

SJ and Olive agreed they'd better just take a quick glance at the old quarters from their vehicle and then continue down Highway 190.

A strange sensation swept over Olive as she gazed over at her old home. Her son was about to merge back on to the highway when a telltale thumping from the rear of the van forced him to apply the brakes, turn off the ignition, and get out to take a look. Sure enough, they weren't going anywhere until the flat tire was changed. Everyone piled out to allow SJ to track down the jack, pull the spare tire off the rear door, and attend to the business of getting his gang back on the road. Olive took her grandsons by the hand, looked both ways up and down the vacant highway, and then walked with them over to the Emigrant ranger station.

Olive was keyed in to the peculiar occurrence that kept them from leaving this place—this place where she and her husband had been enchanted by the quietude of the immense heavens that soared overhead, this place where Stan sang "The Burro Lullaby" to her for the first time, and where their love for each other deepened with each and every star-laden night. She stood there with her grandsons, under the eaves of the front porch where Ranger Stan Jones had sat on a Sunday morning so many years ago and dreamed up the song that had changed their lives. All at once, without a thought, she knew that Stan was there, the chocolate-brown Martin slung over his shoulder with that old piece of rope he used as a strap, laughing and smiling with that ever-present little kid gleam in his eye. Olive's heart swelled as the presence of her husband's bright spirit washed over her like a glaze of golden honey.

Her teenage grandson Davis, sizing up the empty vistas of bare desert and mountains in all directions, wasn't convinced that this was such a cool place. He scanned in through the screened windows at the cramped living quarters, turned to Olive, his face twisted with confusion, and asked, "You lived *here*, Grandma?" Olive, glowing with reverie, smiled gently at her grandson and replied, "Yes, Davis, I lived here."

GHOST RIDERS IN THE SKY

An old cowpoke went riding out one dark and windy day
Upon a ridge he rested as he went along his way
When all at once a mighty herd of red-eyed cows he saw
A ploughin' thru the ragged skies
And up a cloudy draw

Yipi-yi-ay
Yipi-yi-o
The ghost herd in the sky

Their brands were still on fire and their hooves wuz made of steel
Their horns wuz black and shiny and their hot breath he could feel
A bolt of fear went through him as they thundered thru the sky
For he saw the riders comin' hard
And he heard their mournful cry

Yipi-yi-ay
Yipi-yi-o
Ghost Riders in the Sky

Their faces gaunt their eyes were blurred and shirts all soaked with sweat
They're ridin' hard to catch that herd but they ain't caught them yet
'Cause they've got to ride forever on that range up in the sky
On horses snortin' fire
As they ride on hear their cry

Yipi-yi-ay
Yipi-yi-o
Ghost Riders In The Sky

As the riders loped on by him he heard one call his name
If you want to save your soul from hell a-ridin' on our range
Then cowboy change your ways today or with us you will ride
A-try'n to catch the devil's herd
Across these endless skies

Yipi-yi-ay
Yipi-yi-o
The ghost herd in the sky
Ghost Riders in the Sky

(Transcribed from original 1949 sheet music—Edwin H. Morris & Company, Inc.)

ACKNOWLEDGMENTS

THE GENESIS OF THIS BIOGRAPHY STEMS FROM A CALM, STARRY Saturday evening one November at the Furnace Creek Ranch in Death Valley. For many years, the Reinsmen, a stellar western band in the tradition of the Sons of the Pioneers, performed during the Death Valley 49er's Encampment, an annual four-day celebration commemorating a distressed band of pioneers who wandered into the valley in 1849. With dilapidated, old borax wagons as a backdrop, the band always sets up a modest stage for a Saturday night show in the dirt parking lot adjacent to the Furnace Creek General Store, where I happened to be employed through the 1980s.

During these performances, the Reinsmen never failed to play "Ghost Riders in the Sky." When bandleader Dick Goodman introduced the song, he always spoke of "Death Valley Ranger Stan Jones" sitting on the front porch of his ranger station in the 1940s, looking out to see clouds forming over the distant mountains and claimed that Stan "swore he could see those Ghost Riders in the Sky." I was hooked and figured that Stan's years as a national park ranger would be a perfect topic for a paper to present at a Death Valley History Conference held biannually at Furnace Creek.

When I finally began to research Stan's life many years later for the 2008 History Conference, I had two revelations. The first was that there were no substantial biographical accounts written about Stan Jones beyond a few repeated stories about how "Ghost Riders" found its way to Hollywood. The second was that Stan's widow Olive was alive and well and willing to speak with me about her years with Stan in Death Valley.

My conversation with Olive Jones in April of 2006 provided the narrative heart of the paper I presented at Furnace Creek in 2008, which ultimately led to the continued research and writing of this book. I am deeply grateful for the memories Olive shared of her husband and their years together in that remarkable "godforsaken" desert. Many members of the extended Jones clan also generously shared memories, news clippings, and photographs for this book. I want to thank the late Harold Poehlmann, Anne Husmann, the late Bill Dubs, Pam Moritz, Keith Poehlmann, Chris Poehlmann, Ellen Hindman, and Anne Barrett. A rousing yipi-yi-o! goes to Keeter Stuart for facilitating many of my connections with the Jones family.

I am indebted to Cindy Hayostek, long-time resident and premier historian of Douglas, Arizona, for laying the foundation for my account of Stan's early life in and around Douglas, for her sharp editing expertise, and for her gracious support through every step of the way in assisting me to tell this story.

I am extremely grateful for the ease of access and friendly responsiveness exhibited by every single library and research institution I visited or queried for information or photographs germane to this story. These facilities included the Arizona Historical Society; the Cochise County Historical Society; the Douglas Public Library; the Pima County Public Library; Los Angeles Public Library; the Lilly Library of Indiana University; the Inyo County Library; the Eastern California Museum; the Maturango Museum; the Searles Valley Historical Society; the Churchill County Museum of Fallon, Nevada; Special Collections at the University of Southern California Library; the Death Valley National Park Library; and the Mount Rainier National Park Library. Special appreciation is due to Brooke Childrey at Mount Rainier for the efforts she extended to render barely legible mimeographed ranger reports from the 1940s into clean Word documents.

The late Dobe Carey and Johnny Western both cheerfully shared memories of their good pal Stan Jones. I am grateful to Dick Goodman for providing a CD of a 1974 interview conducted by Ken Griffis with Lloyd Perryman, another long-time friend of Stan. Reminiscences of Stan and Olive Jones at Mount Rainier were contributed by Lorraine Larson, Barbara Christianson, Rhoda Pappajohn, Donna Rahier, and Margaret O'Malley. I am especially indebted to Doug Evans who served as my cornerstone for counsel about all things regarding Mount Rainier National Park and Stan's tenure there. Generous assistance regarding Stan and Olive's years in Death Valley were provided by Lynn Keller, Robert Hoshide, David Sprau, Vickie Wolfe, and sisters Myrtle Murchison and Margaret "Lit" Brush, daughters of George and Ann Pipkin. Lit was particularly helpful in sharing photos, newspaper clippings, and her father's written memories of Stan and Olive.

I'd also like to thank Bonnie Lewis, Melinda Carey, Carol Anderson, Brian Chidester, C. L. Yarbrough, Leroy Johnson, Jim Klein, Walter Lonsdale, Robin Bowers, Bonnie Catanzaro, James Drury, Charles Connor, Michelle Sundin, and Kathryn Kalinak for their respective advice, reminiscences, or support. Members of the Vaughn Monroe Society responded immediately when I queried their website and I am very grateful in particular to Jerry Geraldnick who provided me with a rare recording of Vaughn Monroe discussing the origins of "Ghost Riders," along with a link to an interview with Charles Grean, the RCA A&R man responsible for bringing Stan's great song to Monroe's attention. Brent Reed generously shared his father's "Stan Jones" file, which was packed with fabulous photos, promotional materials associated with "Stan Jones Day" in Arizona, and personal letters between his parents and the Joneses, a cumulative gold mine of information that immeasurably enhanced this narrative.

This book benefited terrifically from a talented pack of volunteer editors, all possessed with discerning eyes and frank dispositions. I am keenly appreciative of the time and effort exerted by Bill Broyles, Doug McAdam, Michael Lawson, Don Swann, Douglas B. Green, Brenda Morris, Roger and Peggy Moder, Butch Farabee, and Jeff Nimmo. Every single one of these readers contributed to honing my efforts to a sharper focus. Any factual errors, oversights, or pedestrian writing is solely my responsibility.

A special green and grey thanks to my colleagues at Saguaro National Park, who have been exceedingly obliging over the years in allowing me to moonlight as a biographer. It would have been nigh impossible to write this book without their support. I owe Renaissance cowpoke and photographer extraordinaire Jay Dusard a whale of thanks for bringing my manuscript to the attention of Rio Nuevo Publishers. Everyone at Rio Nuevo has been overwhelmingly supportive: Jim Turner, Deanna Stover, and especially managing editor Aaron Downey, who has exhibited supreme patience with this occasionally feckless first-time author. I would be remiss not to acknowledge and express a deep appreciation to Bonnie Kuykendall and her superb teaching staff at Yoga Vida. During the past few years of writing and researching this book, I've weathered a series of devastating personal losses and family challenges; my yoga practice has been crucial to my efforts to keep my heart calm and my head above water.

Finally, I want to remember and honor the late Linda Devon who was there for me at the very beginning, fortuitously forging a relationship with the Jones family that led directly to my 2006 interview with Olive Jones. Linda continues to hover close by, watching over those of us who are fortunate enough to have been touched by her friendship and generous kindness. Muchas gracious to Linda's sister, Patty Wands, who has cheered and supported my efforts throughout all the years it's taken to complete this project. And lastly, this book would simply not be in your hands were it not for the encouragement and resolute assistance of Pat Grediagin. With deep gratitude and abiding affection, this book is dedicated to her.

NOTES

PROLOGUE

Stan played a tenor guitar. Derived from tenor banjos, the 4-stringed instruments began to be manufactured by the Martin and Gibson guitar makers in the 1920s. Usually tuned CGDA in the style of the banjo that it derived from, many players, including Stan, chose a guitar tuning replicating the standard DGBE of the first four strings of a six-string guitar. http://www.tenorguitar.com/, http://en.wikipedia.org/wiki/Tenor_guitar.

The original published version of Stan's song read "Riders in the Sky (A Cowboy Legend)." Throughout this story, the song will be referenced as either "Riders in the Sky," "Ghost Riders in the Sky," or simply "Ghost Riders."

CHAPTER 1: DOUGLAS, ARIZONA

1 *"One June evening in 1914 . . .":* Reed, Allen C. "Creakin' Leather, Stan Jones—Music Man From Arizona," *Arizona Highways,* October, 1957.

2 *disclosed her bloodlines to George McClellan:* Berta's mother's maiden name was Belle McClellan.

2 *"a bad general and a damn Yankee":* telephone interview with Harold Poehlmann, April 21, 2007.

2 *"We are going to start Sunday School next Sunday":* 18 February, 1906, letter from Nell Jones to John Jones, courtesy of Harold Poehlmann.

2 *"a kind of troubadour":* telephone interview with Harold Poehlmann, April 21, 2007.

5 *"Mr. and Mrs. J. E. Jones of El Paso":* "Miss Jones, Clarence Hinton, Wedded At Episcopal Church Saturday Night," *Douglas International,* December 18, 1922.

6 *"the kind of little boy":* Cindy Hayostek, personal communication.

6 Gladys Acosta's memories are drawn from the *Douglas Daily Dispatch* article, "Recalling Ghost Riders in the Sky," July 27, 1997.

7 *"ideal priest,"* Hayostek, Cindy. *100 Years of History: St. Stephen's Episcopal Church in Douglas, Arizona.* Privately published by St. Stephen's Church.

7 *"I carried the cross":* "Douglas Songwriter Now in Movies Surprised by Growth of Home Town," *Douglas Daily Dispatch,* March 19, 1950.

7 *Introduction To Pageants And Rituals For Cochise Council:* Charles Nichols manuscripts, Arizona Historical Society, Tucson, Arizona.

8 *Hinton's ridiculously oversized sombrero:* "Hinton's Hat Target for Indians": *Douglas Daily Dispatch,* February 26, 1928.

9 *pals Wayne Hester and John Kendricks:* Hayostek, Cindy. *Born In Douglas: Stan Jones and "Ghost Riders in the Sky" Borderland Chronicles No. 2.* Douglas, Arizona: Haystack Publications, 2008.

9 *Stan could often be found huddled over:* James Krentz in Letter to Cindy Hayostek, February 2, 2001.

9 *job as bookkeeper:* Hayostek, Cindy. *Born In Douglas.*

CHAPTER 2: YOUNG RIDERS

11 *Burros, abandoned for the summer months:* "School and Burros Cause Crowded Life For Douglas Youth," *Douglas Daily Dispatch,* October 8, 1929.

11 *Mexican woodcutters*: Hayostek. *Born In Douglas,* 3.

11 *"I've been in many a tough town"*: Hadley, Diana. "Border Boom Town—Douglas, Arizona 1900–1920." *The Cochise Quarterly*, Fall, 1987, p. 24.

11 *"Grandpa's Hill"*: Cindy Hayostek, interview with Lily Maye Hester, September 25, 2006.

12 *"picked up an old guitar"*: Bond, Ervin. "Ghost Riders In The Sky—Stan Jones and Capp Watts" *The Cochise Quarterly*, Summer, Fall 1972, 14.

12 *George Rogers insisted on calling him "Capp"*: Hayostek, *Born In Douglas,* 8.

13 *"long-haired, bearded man on a rock"*: Bond. *Ghost Riders in the Sky,* 10-11.

16 *"To Mom, Who made this song. . ."*: Anne Husmann, telephone communication, January 9, 2012.

CHAPTER 3: IN THE NAVY

19 *Naval recruitment officers*: Military Personnel Records, St. Louis, Missouri, December 22, 2010, Request Number 1-8675536547. These records from Stan's abbreviated stint in the Navy provide the biographical substance for much of this chapter.

20 *help from A.E. Hinton*: "Hinton To Join Gold Rush Mining Camp At Downieville, Calif." *Douglas Daily Dispatch,* June 4, 1932.

20 *"pretty harsh dude"*: Keeter Stuart, personal communication, January 16, 2009.

22 *Bill and Jeanne Dubs drove Berta*: Bill Dubs, telephone interview, January 20, 2012.

22 *Navy heavy cruiser*: USN Ships—USS San Francisco (CA-38), accessed May 3, 2013. http://www.history.navy.mil/photos/sh-usn/usnsh-s/ca38.htm.

22 *He took me for a ride*: personal communication between Keith Poehlmann and Keeter Stuart, January 17, 2009.

22 *Stan and Helen exchanged vows*: Marriage Certificate 8129, Kitsap County, Washington. Washington State Digital Archives. Accessed Dec. 26, 2011.

CHAPTER 4: COWBOY, CHANGE YOUR WAYS

25 *A frisky dalliance*: Anne Barrett, personal communication, December 1, 2010.

25 *A woman named Patsy Fison:* U.S. Navy Personnel Records for Stanley Davis Jones.

26 *A rift between Jeanne and her older brothers*: Bill Dubs, January 12, 2012.

26 *"A lost sheep after the Navy"*: Ibid.

27 *worked for the Forest Service*: Olive Jones, in a letter to Ervin Bond dated January 14, 1972, stated that Stan had indeed worked for the forest service before he was employed by the American Red Cross, but does not specify where, when, or what jobs he may have performed. Letter courtesy of Cindy Hayostek.

27 *Stan had married a woman named Kathryn Johnson*: Marriage Certificate A 3580, Clark County, Washington State. Digital archives accessed January 6, 2012.

27 *In the 1943 divorce decree*: Superior Court of the State of Washington, Clark County, Divorce Decree No. 19232, filed February 9, 1943.

27 *Stan attempted to reenlist*: U.S. Navy Personnel Records for Stanley Davis Jones.

28 *The American Red Cross*: "American Red Cross: Our History." http://www.redcross.org/about-us/history (accessed May 3, 2013).

28 *A cousin of Olive's*: Ellen Hindman, personal correspondence, December 10, 2010.

29 *"If you spent five minutes with my Uncle Stan"*: Harold Poehlmann, April 21, 2007.

30 *Stan's theatrical experience*: "Little Theater To Be Organized at Monday Meet," *The Fallon Eagle,* October 14, 1944.

30 *The future ranger's personal charisma:* "Stanley Jones, Red Cross Field Man, Gets Transfer," *The Fallon Eagle,* December 16, 1944.

31 *skippered by Royal Ingersoll*: Wikipedia, http://en.wikipedia.org/wiki/Royal_E._Ingersoll (accessed May 6, 2013).

31 *Stan played along with his mother's charade that John Jones was somehow still a part of the family:* In a poignant coda to Berta's long life (she died at 96 years of age), her June 21, 1971, obituary in the *Press Democrat of Sonoma County* included "her husband, John" as a survivor. Obituary courtesy of Harold Poehlmann.

CHAPTER 5: MOUNT RAINIER

The majority of Stan's activities as a ranger at Mount Rainier described in this chapter are drawn from the Chief Ranger Monthly Reports. 1945–1946. Courtesy of National Park Service, Mount Rainier National Park.

34 *have a rebellious streak:* Doug Evans, personal communication, March 2006.

34 *A Longmire resident from that era:* Ibid.

35 *A neighbor of Stan and Olive's:* Lorraine Larson, telephone interview, November 10, 2010.

35 *a fire lookout, down from his solitary post:* Ibid.

35 *One ranger recalled the advantage:* Doug Evans, personal communication, December 2, 2008.

37 *A waitress on duty:* Barbara Christianson, telephone interview, February 15, 2009.

38–39 *"Stan had probably composed":* Doug Evans, personal communication, March, 2006.

CHAPTER 6: A HOT, MISERABLE, GODFORSAKEN HOLE

A personal interview with Olive Jones on April 16, 2006, at her home in Tarzana, California, provided the heart of the narrative recounting the years that she and her husband spent living in Death Valley.

Many of the incidents described and quoted in the following chapters are derived from the Superintendent Monthly Reports. 1946–1949. Courtesy of National Park Service. Death Valley National Park.

43 *The Goodwin years:* Quote from Matt Ryan taken from *Theodore R. Goodwin—Keepsake No.18* (published by Death Valley '49ers, 1978), 20.

45 *"The Songbird of Wildrose":* Margaret Brush, personal communication, July 11, 2007.

47 *Saturday night square dances:* L. Lynn Keller, *A River Runner's Life* (Published by author, 2011).

47 *burro eradication program:* Hal K. Rothman, *Draft Administrative History of Death Valley National Park.* Courtesy of National Park Service, Death Valley National Park.

50 *One winter day, Stan and his deputy sheriff pal:* George Pipkin, *Desert Sands; Stories of the Mojave Desert and the Death Valley Country* (Published by author, 1964), 43.

50 *Stan's innate bravura:* Ibid., 41.

52 *George Palmer Putnam, a good friend:* "Cameo of George Palmer Putnam." *Historical Society of the Upper Mojave Desert Newsletter,* June 2006.

54 *"no stars forgot to shine":* William Manly, *Death Valley In '49* (Bishop, CA: Chalfant Press, 1977).

CHAPTER 7: NO WATER IN THAT CACTUS

Many of the incidents described and quoted in this chapter are derived from the Superintendent's Monthly Reports. 1946–1949. Courtesy of National Park Service. Death Valley National Park.

55 *She recollects that this was in 1947:* Margaret Brush. personal communication, November 8, 2011.

58 *Ward Bond's obsession:* Harry Carey Jr., *Company of Heroes* (Lanham, MD: Madison Books, 1996), 29.

58 *acceptable boundaries that a film crew:* "Cave Paintings for Film Attacked." *Los Angeles Times,* April 24, 2000, http://articles.latimes.com/1990-04-26/news/mn-324_1_state-park-cavern.

58 *Ranger Jones was on hand for a scene:* Carey, *Company of Heroes,* 34–36.

59 *George Palmer Putnam personally escorted*: "Columbia Shooting Major Production at Stove Pipe Wells," *Inyo Independent,* May 21, 1948.

CHAPTER 8: NATURE BOY

Much of the information related in this chapter is derived from the Superintendent Monthly Reports. 1946–1949. Courtesy of National Park Service, Death Valley National Park.

63 *Helen Ogston recalled her reaction*: Interview with Helen Ogston by Walter Rudolph. KBYU, National Public Radio, Provo, Utah. Courtesy of Vicki Wolfe.

64 *(Years later lead singer Bob Nolan)*: Dick Goodman, personal communication, December 22, 2005.

64 *Stan had also received an offer*: "Death Valley Park Ranger Hits Song Jackpot; Numerous Numbers Hailed." *Inyo Independent,* February 4, 1949.

64 *Presto direct-to-disc recorder*: "Presto!" *The New Yorker,* April 9, 2012, 73.

65 *In an extraordinary 1948 interview*: The video footage of the interview with Eden Ahbez on, *We The People,* may be found on http://www.shadowboxstudio.com/edenahbez.htm.

67 *"I have a song I think you'll like"*: Notes from the sheet music of "Riders in the Sky: A Cowboy Legend." Edwin H. Morris & Company, Inc., 1949.

68 *the Joneses received a letter:* Olive Jones. Personal Interview, April 16, 2006.

CHAPTER 9: ALL THE STARS OF DEATH VALLEY

Superintendent Monthly Reports. 1946–1949. Courtesy of National Park Service. Death Valley National Park.

71 *"I went home and played it"*: Burl Ives interview, *San Antonio Light,* October 16, 1949.

72 *In a highly unusual foreword*: Notes from the sheet music of "Riders in the Sky: A Cowboy Legend. Edwin H. Morris & Company, Inc., 1949.

73 *Bandleader and vocalist Vaughn Monroe*: Escott, Colin. *The Very Best of Vaughn Monroe,* Taragon Records, Compact Disc liner notes, 1998.

74 *Monroe hit pay dirt*: Interview with Charles Green. Streissguth, Michael. http://home.comcast.net/~bruce.comer/green.htm (accessed May 7, 2013).

78 *Eleanor Roosevelt, in her daily letter*: "My Day, by Eleanor Roosevelt," May 21, 1949. http://www.gwu.edu/~erpapers/myday/displaydoc.cfm?_y=1949&_f=md001285. Accessed May 7, 2013.

CHAPTER 10: WE HOPE HE MAKES A MILLION DOLLARS

Superintendent Monthly Reports. 1946–1949. Courtesy of National Park Service. Death Valley National Park.

83 *Billboard magazine reported*: "WM Inks Jones To Term Paper," *Billboard,* May 21, 1949, http://books.google.com/ (accessed May 9, 2013).

84 *A brief review in Billboard*: *Billboard,* June 4, 1949, 123. Folk Charts. http://books.google.com/ (accessed May 9, 2013).

84 *On one trip to Hollywood*: "Turning Point; A lucky meeting was worth $100,000 plus," *Parade: The Sunday Picture Magazine,* December 10, 1950.

85 *Stan's response*: Chris Poehlmann, personal communication with Linda Devon, June 5, 2005.

86 *Pipkin captured the strained denouement*: Pipkin, George. *Desert Sands; Stories of the Mojave Desert and the Death Valley Country.* (Published by author, 1964), 44.

86 *A Midwesterner remembers*: Leroy Johnson, personal communication, February 8, 2008.

86 *A pious Detroit disc jockey*: "Give 'Em Ned, Ed!" *Billboard*, June 18, 1949, 20. http://books.google.com/ (accessed May 9, 2013).

87 *Even livestock couldn't escape*: Donna Rahier, from a story told her by former Mount Rainier employee, Forrest Johnson, personal communication, August 20, 2009.

87 *RCA Victor continued its massive promotional push*: "Riders Still Riding High In The Sales Sky," *RCA Victor Record Bulletin*, June 20, 1949, Author's Collection.

88 *After a performance at the Oriental Theater*: Vaudeville Reviews. *Billboard*, July 30, 1949, 21.

88 *Stan's great friend and fellow musician*: Johnny Western's memories of Stan Jones were recorded during a phone interview with the author on March 24, 2011.

88 *Lloyd Perryman, a longtime member of the Sons of the Pioneers*: Lloyd Perryman interview recorded in 1974 by Ken Griffis. Courtesy of Dick Goodman.

89 *Autry already had in production*: Holly George-Warren, *Public Cowboy No.1; The Life and Times of Gene Autry*. (Oxford; New York: Oxford University Press, 2007), 255.

91 *Olive wrote a note*: Letter from Olive Jones to Ann Pipkin. Courtesy of Margaret Brush.

CHAPTER 11: DON'T WRITE ANYTHING ABOUT CACTUS!

The account of the "reunion" of Stan Jones and John Ford is drawn from Harry Carey Jr., *Company of Heroes*. (Lanham, Maryland: Taylor Trade Publishing, Copyright 2013 The Carey Living Trust, p. 91–94), and the liner notes "Excerpts from a conversation with Harry Carey Jr.", from the soundtrack of *Rio Grande*. Varese Sarabande Records, VSD-5378, 1993.

95 *"the movie threatened to become a Stan Jones concert"*: Scott Eyman. *Print The Legend: The Life and Times of John Ford* (New York, Simon & Schuster, 1999), 366.

96 *"Uncle Jack always said Wagon Master"*: Carey. *Company of Heroes*. (Lanham, MD: Taylor Trade Publishing, The Carey Living Trust, 2013),107.

97–98 Quotes from Stan are drawn from "Douglas Songwriter Now in Movies Surprised by Growth of Home Town," *Douglas Daily Dispatch*, March 19, 1950.

99 *Walt was on the air introducing Stan*: YouTube video accessed February 12, 2011. http://www.youtube.com/watch?v=ne67mdMDHw8 (currently not available).

99 *Stan was still a ranger*: "Desert Sands, by George Pipkin," *Trona Argonaut*, February 12, 1948.

99 *The national press first mentions*: "Riding High," *Newsweek*, May 2, 1949, 80.

99 *Vaughn Monroe recorded a special promotional disc*: I am grateful to Jerry Geraldnick of the Vaughn Monroe Society (http://www.vaughnmonroesociety.org/) for sending me a CD copy of this interview from the original 78 disc.

99 *In a radio interview conducted by Lloyd Perryman*: Sons of the Pioneers. *Memories of "Lucky U" Ranch*. Jasmine Records, JASMCD 3528, 2002.

100 *Dobe Carey observed*: telephone conversation with Dobe Carey, March 12, 2007.

100 *once told a friend*: telephone conversation with Johnny Western, February 24, 2011.

101 *Beverly Hillbillies radio show in Los Angeles*: "Wildrose Café Man Tells of Stan Jones," *Rocketeer*, China Lake, California, July 19, 1950. Courtesy of Margaret Brush.

101 Carey *recalled Ford's petulant tactics*: Carey, *Company of Heroes*, 108.

102 *O'Brien's son, Darcy, recalled*: Ronald R. Davis. *John Ford: Hollywood's Old Master*. (Norman, OK: University of Oklahoma Press, 1995), 230.

CHAPTER 12: SILVER SCREEN SONGWRITER

105 *Hedda Hopper continued to keep tabs*: "Jeffery Lynn Will Star in 'Forty Notches'", Hedda Hopper, *Los Angeles Times*, December 2, 1950.

105 *He had composed an operetta*: "Filmland Briefs," *Los Angeles Times*, May 31, 1950.

106 *Stan also gained permission in 1951*: "Drama," Hedda Hopper, *Los Angeles Times*, June 18, 1951.

106 *A song described as a "Kentucky folk tune"*: "Movieland Briefs," *Los Angeles Times,* October 28, 1952.

107 *They had a beautiful place*: Telephone interview with Dobe Carey, March 12, 2007.

107 *A nephew of Stan's attending the University of Nevada*: personal communication between Keith Poehlmann and Keeter Stuart, January 16, 2009. Courtesy of Keeter Stuart.

107 *family journeyed to Crystal Bay*: Telephone interview with Bill Dubs, January 20, 2012.

108 *received a hero's welcome*: Ellen Hindman, personal communication with author, December 16, 2010.

109 *"Stan could tell a good joke"*: Harold Poehlmann, telephone conversation with author, April 21, 2007.

109 *Johnny Western attests*: Johnny Western, telephone interview, March 24, 2011.

109 *Lloyd Perryman was duly impressed:* Lloyd Perryman interview with Ken Griffis, 1974.

109 *Dobe described the strategy*: Dobe Carey, telephone interview, March 12, 2007.

109 *He quoted lyrics written by Stan*: Harry Carey Jr. *Company of Heroes,* 160.

110 *a "wonderful" marriage:* Dobe Carey, telephone interview, March 12, 2007.

110 *"always a challenge and always interesting"*: Michelle Sundin, "Stanley Davis 'Stan' Jones", http://www.bobnolan-sop.net/index.htm.

110 *"everyone was stewed every night"*: Dobe Carey's memories are drawn from telephone interview with author, March 12, 2007.

110 *Stan offered his talent*: "12 Film Figures to Aid in Public Service Shows," *Los Angeles Times,* April 20, 1953.

CHAPTER 13: I'M NO ACTOR

116 *Berta could barely stand to be observed*: Harold Poehlmann, phone interview April 21, 2007.

117 *a rather prosaic review in the Los Angeles Times*: "Brentwood Players Act Out 'Night Must Fall,'" *Los Angeles Times,* May 30, 1956.

117 *Francis Lyon . . . took an interest*: "Drama," *Los Angeles Times,* May 31, 1956.

117 *Olive shared the news*: Letter from Olive Jones to Allen and Shirley Reed. Courtesy of Brent Reed.

118 *Originally touted in the press*: Walter Ames, *Los Angeles Times,* October 1, 1956.

118 *Entertainment columnist Walter Ames*: Ibid.

119 *"I'm no actor"*: Stan Jones, liner notes for *Songs of the National Parks,* Disneyland Records, WDL-1005, 1958.

119 *the thrill of visiting "Uncle Stan"*: Keeter Stuart, personal communication, March 4, 2011.

120 *Stan, John Bromfield, and their smiling spouses*: "TV Stars Greeted By Gun Serenade," *Douglas Daily Dispatch,* March 29, 1957.

120 *"both men addressed students . . ."*: Ibid.

121 *in an article previewing his arrival*: "TV Series Author Arriving For Rodeo," *Douglas Daily Dispatch,* March 28, 1957.

122 *he confessed to the Los Angeles Times*: "John Bromfield, *Wikipedia.* Accessed May13, 2013. http://en.wikipedia.org/wiki/John_Bromfield.

CHAPTER 14: CREAKIN' LEATHER

127 *Stan had been asked by the staff at the Disney Music Department*: The "biography" Stan Jones wrote for the Disney staff courtesy of Brent Reed.

129 *writer and photographer responsible for the article, Allen Reed*: letters between the Joneses and the Reeds and promotional material for Stan Jones Day courtesy of Brent Reed.

CHAPTER 15: SONG OF THE TRAIL

135 *dinner with park ranger Doug Evans*: Doug Evans, personal communication, April 2006.

135 *Stan taught them the words to "Ghost Riders"*: Rhoda Pappajohn, personal communication,

November 21, 2010.

139 *In an August, 1958, letter*: courtesy of Western Archaeology Conservation Center, Tucson, Arizona.

CHAPTER 16: ROLL ALONG

143 *"who in the heck . . . ?"*: Harold Poehlmann, telephone interview, April 21, 2007.

143 *Stan telegrammed*: Contents of telegram and accounts of Bud Molinek's friendship with Stan Jones courtesy of Margaret O'Malley, personal communication.

144 *Stan got a call from a young woman*: Anne Barrett, personal communication, January 5, 2011.

144 *she remembered a relaxed scene*: Anne Barrett, personal communication, February 20, 2012.

145 *Stan's great-nephew, Keeter*: Keeter Stuart, personal communication, March 5, 2011.

145–146 *a congratulatory letter sent by Olive*: letter from Olive Jones to Allen and Shirley Reed dated January 11, 1960. Courtesy of Brent Reed.

147 *Drury erroneously believed*: James Drury, telephone interview with author, January 14, 2012.

147 *Stan created a small-town frenzy*: The information that chronicles Stan's visit to Petaluma is drawn from a *Petaluma Argus Courier* clipping provided courtesy of Harold Poehlmann, dated solely as 1960.

148 *Stan dutifully appeared*: "Coyotes' Defenders Speak Out at Animal Regulation Hearing," *Los Angeles Times,* October 2, 1960.

149 *Stan warrants his own biography*: The Original Mickey Mouse Club Show. http://www.originalmmc.com/stanjones.html.

151 *America Sings*: Courtesy of Keeter Stuart.

CHAPTER 17: YOU NEVER REALLY EVER DIED

153 *Producer-arranger Joe Leahy's newly formed label*: "Leahy Picks Allied World-Wide Outlet For His New Label," *Billboard,* March 13, 1961. http://books.google.com/books (accessed May 14, 2013).

153 *Referred to by Stan*: Liner notes, *Walter Brennan: By The Fireside,* Record Producers Corporation, RPC-M106.

158 *According to Dobe Carey*: Author interview with Carey.

158 *Perryman recalled his final visit*: Lloyd Perryman interview with Ken Griffis, 1974.

158 *Johnny Western could not believe*: Author interview with Western.

159 *Written by the Joneses' good friend*: Text for the tribute to Stan read by George Putnam, courtesy of Harold Poehlmann.

159 *In a typed letter to Stan's mother*: Letter written by Olive Jones, courtesy of Harold Poehlmann.

160 *Johnny Western remained confounded*: Author interview with Western.

161 *the following letter*: Courtesy of Brent Reed.

CHAPTER 18: GHOST RIDERS IN THE SKY

164 *one of their most popular songs:* Charles Conner, personal communication, January 23, 2012.

165 *roughly a third are instrumentals*: C. L. Yarbough, personal communication, December 14, 2012.

165 *The surname Watts has Germanic roots*: "Last name: Watts," *Surname Database,* accessed January 25, 2012. http://www.surnamedb.com/.

165 *The gist of the grim scenario*: "Orkneyjar—The Wild Hunt," accessed November 11, 2010, http://www.orkneyjar.com/tradition/hunt.htm._

165 *those who witness the ghastly procession*: Ibid.

165–166 *Vaughn Monroe recorded a special promotional disc*: I am grateful to Jerry Geraldnick of the Vaughn Monroe Society (http://www.vaughnmonroesociety.org/) for sending me a CD copy of this interview from the original 78 disc.

166 *"Old cowpunchers say"*: John R. Craddock, *Chronicles of Oklahoma,* accessed November 22, 2010, http://digital.library.okstate.edu/Chronicles/v002/v002p269.html.

167 *"Well, I saw the ghost herd"*: Elmer Ping, http://www.homestead.com, accessed January 28, 2012.

167 *"To William"*: courtesy of Bill Dubs.

168 *Sons of the Pioneers reportedly passed"*: Dick Goodman, personal communication, December 22, 2005.

168 *Johnny Western recalls*: Author interview with Western.

169 *When Morris was inducted*: Songwriters Hall of Fame—1994 Award and Induction Ceremony, http://www.songwritershalloffame.org (accessed November 7, 2010).

170 *"Olive hated his version"*: Author interview with Johnny Western.

171 *He attributed the magic feel*: Keeter Stuart, personal communication, March 5, 2011.

EPILOGUE

Olive Jones, personal interview, Tarzana, California, April 16, 2006.

SUGGESTED READING

Bond, Ervin. "Ghost Riders In The Sky—Stan Jones and Capp Watts." *The Cochise Quarterly* 2, nos. 2 & 3 (Summer/ Fall 1972) 9–16.

Carey Jr., Harry. *Company of Heroes.* Lanham, MD: Taylor Trade Publishing, 2013.

Cowie, Peter. *John Ford And The American West.* New York: Abrams, 2004.

D'Arc, James V. *When Hollywood Came To Town: A History of Movie Making in Utah.* Layton, UT: Gibbs Smith, 2010.

Eyman, Scott. *Print The Legend: The Life and Times of John Ford.* New York: Simon & Schuster, 1999.

Farabee Jr., Charles R. "Butch." *National Park Ranger: An American Icon.* Lanham, MD: Roberts Rhinehart Publishers, 2003.

Frankel, Glenn. *The Searchers: The Making of an American Legend.* New York: Bloomsbury USA, 2013.

George-Warren, Holly. *Cowboy: How Hollywood Invented the Wild West.* U.K.: Ivy Press Limited, 2002.

Goodwin, Neville, and Neil Goodwin, *Apache Diaries: A Father-Son Journey.* Lincoln: University of Nebraska Press, 2000.

Green, Douglas B. *Singing in the Saddle: The History of the Singing Cowboy.* Nashville: Vanderbilt University Press and the Country Music Foundation Press, 2002.

Hadley, Diana. "Border Boom Town—Douglas, Arizona 1900–1920." *The Cochise Quarterly* 17, no. 3 (Fall 1987).

Hayostek, Cindy *Born In Douglas: Stan Jones and "Ghost Riders in the Sky," Borderland Chronicles No. 2.* Douglas, AZ: Haystack Publications, 2008.

———, *Douglas.* Mount Pleasant, SC: Arcadia Publishing, 2009.

Hilburn, Robert. *Johnny Cash: The Life.* New York: Little, Brown, and Company, 2013.

Kalinak, Kathryn. *How The West Was Sung: Music In The Westerns of John Ford.* Berkeley, University of California Press, 2007.

———, Editor. *Music in the Western: Notes From The Frontier.* New York: Routledge, 2012.

Manly, William Lewis. *Death Valley In '49.* Bishop, CA: Chalfant Press, 1977.

Pipkin, George. *Desert Sands; Stories of the Mojave Desert and the Death Valley Country.* Published by author, 1964.

Tinsley, Joe Bob. *For A Cowboy Has To Sing.* Gainesville: University of Central Florida Press, 1991.

Utley, Robert. *Clash of Cultures: Fort Bowie and the Chiricahua Apaches.* Washington: Office of Publications, National Park Service, 1977.

Walker, Ardis, Horace Albright, and Ron Miller. *Theodore R. Goodwin: Death Valley '49ers Keepsake No. 18.* Pasadena, CA: Castle Press, 1978.

Williams, John R. *This Was Your Hit Parade.* Rockland, ME: Courier-Gazette, Inc., 1973.

DISCOGRAPHY

All of the following record albums have long been out of print and remain difficult to find. *Creakin' Leather* has been re-issued as a digital album on the Buena Vista label with the new title, *Ghost Riders in the Sky,* and is available on many music download sites.

Brennan, Walter. *By The Fireside.* Record Producers Corporation, RPC-M106.

Jones, Stan. *America Sings: A Program of Folk Songs of Our Land.* Allied Record Manufacturing Company, Program No. 8.

_____. *Creakin' Leather.* Walt Disney Music Company, WDL-3015.

_____. *Songs of the National Parks: Stan Jones and the Ranger Chorus.* Walt Disney Music Company, WDL-1005.

_____. *This Was The West: The Story and The Songs by Stan Jones.* Walt Disney Music Company, WDL-3033.

_____. *"I Am An American": School Broadcast Selections By Stan Jones.* Capitol Records, Inc., Custom Services Department, 1962.

COMPACT DISCS

Johnny Western and The Sons of the Pioneers. *Have Gun, Will Travel.* C.D.C.C., Inc. 270304.11, 2004. There are six Stan Jones songs on this fine album, including "The Searchers" and "Cowpoke."

Monroe, Vaughn. *The Very Best of Vaughn Monroe.* Taragon Records, TARCD-1032, 1998.

Sons of the Pioneers. *Memories of "Lucky U" Ranch.* Jasmine Records, JASMCD 3528, 2002.

Stuart, Keeter. *Ghost Riders, Searchers, & Cowpokes: The Timeless Songs of Stan Jones.* Keeter Stuart, 2008. http://www.keeterstuart.com/

Young, Victor. *Rio Grande.* Soundtrack from the John Ford film. Varese Sarabande Records, VSD-5378, 1993.

WEB LINKS

www.bobnolan-sop.net/index.htm

The best comprehensive collection of songs written by Stan Jones may be heard on the Bob Nolan website that Ranger Doug of Riders In The Sky has lauded in his foreword to this book. Click on "biographies," choose Stan Jones, and you will be treated to the diverse range of Stan's talents as a songwriter. Included is a link to Stan telling his story to Lloyd Perryman of how he was inspired to write "Ghost Riders."

http://bcxists.wordpress.com

This is a blog about all things Eden Ahbez, a fascinating character who played a serendipitous role in Stan Jones's destiny.

gritsencats@gmail.com

Curious about the multitude of covers recorded of "Ghost Riders in the Sky" over the past sixty-five years? This email address will connect you with a gentleman, C. L. Yarbrough, who has made it his mission to seek out every version of the song ever recorded. He has set up this address specifically to communicate with other "Ghost Riders" aficionados. Yipi-yi-o!

The Adventures of Spin and Marty: The Mickey Mouse Club. Walt Disney Treasures, K5732.

This collection of the first season of the *Spin and Marty* serial contains the only television footage I've been able to locate of Stan Jones singing and playing his tenor guitar.

Ten Who Dared. Walt Disney Studios Home Entertainment, 2009.

Stan is featured playing his guitar in a scene by the campfire as James Drury and Ben Johnson lip-synch the Stan Jones composition "Roll Along." This is the sole feature film footage available of Stan playing his guitar.

U.S. Marshall: John Bromfield. TV Classic Westerns, Echo Bridge Home Entertainment, 2003.

A number of episodes featuring Stan as Deputy Harry Olsen are included in this collection.

INDEX

A

Acosta, Gladys, 6
"Adventures of Spin and Marty, The," 115
Ahbez, Eden, 64–67, 71, 84–85, 90
"Ain't Nature Boy Grand; Eden Spurs Riders in the Sky" *(Billboard),* 72
Almanac Singers, 71
"Along the Yellowstone" (song by Jones), 138
American Music Company, 64
American Red Cross, 28, 30
America Sings radio program, 151, 152
Ames, Walter, 118
Apache Indians, 7–8, 11–12, 128
Argosy Pictures, 55
Arizona
    appreciation of, 131, 132, 146, 152
    promotional events in, 119–122, 129–132
Arizona Highways, 129, 131
Armendáriz, Pedro, 56–57
Arnaz, Desi, 120
Autry, Gene, 89, 105–106

B

Barrett, Anne, 144–145
Baxter, Anne, 61–62
Bender, H. G., 35
Bergfield, George A., 20, 97
Bergman, Ingmar, 56
Beumler, Henry, 120
Beyond the Purple Hills, 89
"Beyond the Purple Hills" (song by Jones), 64
"Big Scoop about Jones, The," *(Petaluma Argus Courier),* 148
Big Sky, The, 106
Billboard, 72, 74, 83–84, 87
Bond, Ervin, 13, 14
Bond, Ward, 56–58
Boone, Richard, 168
borax mining in Death Valley, 42–43
Bowden, Percy, 160
Boy Scout Handbook, 8
Boy Scouts of America, 7, 8
Brennan, Andrew, 156

Brennan, Walter, 153–156
Bromfield, John, 118, 120, 122
Brown, Harry Joe, 59–60
Brush, Margaret, 55
burro eradication program in Death Valley, 47, 69
"Burro Lullaby, The," (song by Jones), 48, 52, 55, 88, 127, 152, 171
By The Fireside (album by Jones), 153–156

C

cactus, 58–59, 95
Calvary Cemetery (Douglas, Arizona), 15, 97, 158
Camp Victorio, Arizona, 7
Cananea Consolidated Copper Company, 2
Cantor, Eddie, 87
Capitol Records, 64
Carey, Jr., Harry "Dobe"
    acting roles of, 56–59, 95, 116, 149
    Company of Heroes, 56–57, 109–110
    Jones and, 93–95, 100, 101, 102, 107, 109, 158
    Olive's humor and, 110
Carey, Sr., Harry, 56
Cash, Johnny, 163, 169, 170–171
"Cattle Call" (song by Jones), 88
"Cause I'm In Love" (song by Jones), 107
Chapman, Oscar L., 106
Charles, Patricia, 147
Cheyenne, 117
Children of Bodom, 163
Clarke, Jeanie, 144
Cochise County Historical Society Journal, 14
Cole, Nat King, 57–58, 64–66
Collins, Judy, 163
Columbia Pictures, 55, 59
Columbia Records, 71–72
Company of Heroes (Carey), 56–57, 109–110
Copper Queen Smelter, 2, 3, 4, 5
"Cottonwood Tree" (song by Jones), 151
"Cowpoke" (song by Jones), 55, 88, 142, 151, 171

coyote trapping in Tarzana, 148–149
Creakin' Leather (album by Jones), 24, 123, 125–133, 142, 151, 171
"Creakin' Leather" (song by Jones), 125
Crosby, Bing, 74
Curtis, Ken, 101

D

Davis, Berta Margaret. *See* Jones, Berta Davis (mother)
Davis, Grover (uncle), 2, 3, 4
Davis, Jeff, 128
Dear Old Cochise: A Pageant in Three Acts, 8
Death Valley National Monument
    about, 41–42, 44, 53–54
    Easter service in, 68–69
    Emigrant Ranger Station, vii, 45–46
    management of, 43, 49
    movie industry in, 55–62
    songs composed in, 48, 52, 55, 127
"Deep Water" (song by Jones), 24, 125–126, 155
Deer Cliff Inn, 108
"Desert, The," (song by Jones), 138
Desilu Productions, 118, 120, 122
Disney, Walt, 99, 113, 122–123, 126, 128, 129, 130
Disneyland Records, 123, 129, 135–142
Douglas, Arizona, 1, 2, 3, 5, 11, 97–98, 118–122
Douglas Daily Dispatch, 18–19, 97–98, 121, 156
Dragon, Carmen, 149
Drury, James, 146, 147
Dubs, Bill (nephew), 107–108, 167
Dubs, Jeanne Jones. *See* Jones, Jeanne (sister)
Dubs, William, 17, 20, 21

E

Earp, Wyatt, 100
Edwin H. Morris and Company, 72, 169
Emigrant Ranger Station (Death Valley National Monument), vii, 45–46
Erie Cattle Company, 12
Evans, Doug, 34, 135

F

Fallon Eagle, The, 30
Fison, Patsy, 25–26
Ford, Barbara, 101
Ford, John, 56–59, 93–97, 101–102
Foreman, Bob and Mary, 80

Fort Apache, 93
Furnace Creek Inn & Ranch, 42, 47, 50, 53, 56, 57, 61, 67

G

"Geisterreiter," 164
Gene Autry Productions, 89
Geronimo, 8, 11–12, 142
Ghost Rider (film, 2007), 163–164
Ghost Riders, Searchers & Cowpokes: The Timeless Songs of Stan Jones, 171
"Ghost Riders" (song version by Ramrods), 170
"Ghost Riders" (song version in Waila), 164
"Ghost Riders in the Sky" (song by Jones)
    complete lyrics of, 175
    cow's reaction to, 87
    film production rights of, 89
    inspiration for, 13–15, 98, 99–100, 165–167, 168–169, 172
    instrumental versions of, 164, 170
    legacy of, vii, 127, 163–165
    media attention for, 72, 74, 76–79, 97–98
    performances by Jones, 55, 61, 62, 88, 102
    quotes about, 72, 74, 78–79, 164, 168
    recording of, 63–64, 68, 71–72, 74
    review of, 64, 71, 72
    sheet music of, 63–64, 73, 169–170
    versions of
        by Bing Crosby, 74–75
        by Burl Ives, 71–72, 74, 75, 87, 170
        by Children of Bodom, 163
        by Frank Sinatra, 81
        by Johnny Cash, 163, 169, 170–171
        by Judy Collins, 163
        by Keeter Stuart, 171–172
        by Mary McCaslin, 163
        by Pedro Vargas, 75
        by Peggy Lee, 75
        by Ramrods, 170
        by San Francisco Gay Men's Chorus, 163
        by Sons of the Pioneers, 75, 87
        by Spiderbait, 163–164
        by Spike Jones, 75
        by Traveling Wilburys, 163
        by Vaughn Monroe, 74, 86, 87, 170
Goodwin, Theodore R.
    about, 41, 43, 44
    impressions of Jones's success, 67, 68, 75–76, 83, 85, 86
    reports by, 49, 55–56, 59, 69

"Grand Canyon" (song by Jones), 138
Grean, Charles, 74, 170
Great Locomotive Chase, The, 116, 117, 137
Greaves, Katherine, 28
Greaves, Olive. *See* Jones, Olive Greaves
    (third wife)
Greaves, Oliver, 28

H

"Hannah Lee" (song by Jones), 111
Hannah Lee: An American Primitive, 111
Have Gun Will Travel, 168
Heckman, William, 39
Hester, Wayne, 9, 12, 143
High Noon, 106
Hinton, A. E., 5–6, 8, 15
Hinton, Clara Jones. *See* Jones, Clara (sister)
Hinton, Clarence (brother-in-law), 5, 6,
    15, 27
"Hitch-Hiker, The," (story by Jones), 18–19
Honorary Sheriff of Tarzana, 149
Hopper, Hedda, 95, 96, 105, 110, 153
Horse Soldiers, The, 113, 116
Howard, Jack, 120

I

I Am An American (album by Jones), 149, 161
"Indian Spirit Chant" (song by Jones), 141
Ingersoll, Royal, 31
Inman, Jerry, 160–161
"In The Shadows of my Heart" (song by
    Jones), 126
*Introduction To Pageants and Rituals For
    Cochise Council* (Nichols), 7
Inyo Independent, 67–68
Ireland, John, 110–111
Iron Horse, 93
Ives, Burl, 67, 68, 71–72, 74, 75, 87, 170

J

Jesse James' Women, 111–112
Jim and Rita Donnelly, 68
"Jim Marshall's Nugget" (song by Jones), 141
"Jinetes En El Cielo," 75, 164
Johnson, Ben, 94–95, 107, 146
Johnson, Kathryn. *See* Jones, Kathryn
    Johnson (second wife)
Jones, Berta Davis (mother), 1–6, 9, 16, 17,
    116, 127, 145, 159
Jones, Clara (sister), 2–6, 8, 15, 18, 27
Jones, Davis Walsh (son), 26–27, 128

Jones, Helen Walsh (first wife), 22–23,
    26–27, 123
Jones, Jack (brother), 2–5, 20, 26
Jones, Jeanne (sister), 2–5, 17, 26
Jones, Jonathon Edmund (father), 1–4, 6,
    26, 31, 99, 118, 127, 152, 166
Jones, Kathryn Johnson (second wife), 27
Jones, Malcomb (brother), 2–5, 26
Jones, Molly Anne (daughter), 26–27, 128
Jones, Nancy Kay (daughter), 27
Jones, Nell (sister), 2–4, 17
Jones, Olive Greaves (third wife)
    Carey and humor of, 110
    in Death Valley, 44, 53–54
    description of, 132, 144
    family of, 108
    letter to Berta, 159–160
    Life article and, 77
    marriage with Jones, 28–31, 40, 110
    pregnancy of, 145–146
    support of Jones's work, 63, 170–171
Jones, Spike, 74, 75
Jones, Stan, Jr., 145–146, 155–156, 160
Jones, Stanley Davis
    acting roles of, 101, 105, 106, 115, 117,
        118–120, 142, 143, 146, 149
    albums by
        Creakin' Leather, 24, 123, 125–133,
            142, 151, 171
        By The Fireside, 153–156
        I Am An American, 149
        Songs of the National Parks, 133,
            135–142
        This Was The West, 141
    alcohol and smoking by, 108, 110, 158
    biographical fabrications of, 31, 99, 100,
        118, 127–129, 136
    book projects by, 117, 118, 121, 143, 148
    charity work of, 107, 109, 110, 143,
        149, 151
    childhood of, vii, 1, 4–6, 127–128
    children of, 25–27, 26–27, 144
    death of, 158–159
    descriptions of, 20, 21, 26, 34, 88, 94,
        108–109, 136
    employment of, 9, 19–20, 30, 34, 149–151
    film by, 117
    health of, 6, 22, 23–24, 158–159, 161
    magazine articles on, 72, 74, 76–79,
        86–87, 90, 95, 96–97, 99
    marriages of, 22, 25–27, 30, 110 (*See also*

Jones, Olive Greaves (third wife))
  as miner, 20
  named Honorary Sheriff of Tarzana, 149
  newspaper articles on, 95, 96, 97–98,
    105, 118, 121, 148
  performances by, 19, 108, 135, 151
  plays by, 105–106, 149
  quotes by, 77, 90, 96–97, 99–101,
    119, 125
  rescue missions by, 38, 50–52
  schooling of, 19–20
  songs by (*See* "Ghost Riders in the Sky"
    (song by Jones); *specific titles*)
  storytelling, 6, 11–12, 31
  works by (*See specific titles*)
  writings by, 19–20, 34

K

Kendricks, John, 9, 12

L

Lake Tahoe, California, 91, 107
Lange, Henry J., 159
Larson, Lorraine, 35
Last Musketeer, The, 106
Lava, William, 117
Leahy, Joe, 153
Lee, Peggy, 75
"Legend of Stampede Mesa," 165, 166, 167
Legend of the Woodland Bells (operetta by
  Jones), 105–106
Life (magazine), 76–77
"Lilies Grow High, The," (song by Jones),
  109–110, 142, 156, 160, 171
Lilies Grow High, The, (book project by
  Jones), 117, 121, 148
"Little Son" (song by Jones), 156
Los Angeles, California, 17, 20. *See also*
  Tarzana, California
Los Angeles Times, 86, 117, 118, 122,
  148–149

M

Marshal's Daughter, The, 107
Martin, C. W., 20
McCaslin, Mary, 163
McClellan, George, 2
McFarland, Ernest W., 129, 130
"Mean So Much To Me" (song by Jones), 126
Mickey Mouse Club, 116, 149
Miller, Frank, 109

Moab, Utah, 94–96
Molinek, Bud, 143–144
Monroe, Vaughn, 73–74, 86, 87, 99, 166, 170
Morris, Edwin "Buddy," 72, 75, 169
Morris, William, 83
Mount Rainier National Park, 33–40
movie industry, 55–62, 89, 93–97,
  101–102, 106–107. *See also specific titles*
"My Gal is Purple" (song by Jones), 102

N

National Park Service, 34, 36–38, 49–50,
  58–59, 62, 137, 139
Nat King Cole Trio, 66
"Nature Boy," 57–58, 64–66, 85
Newsweek, 76, 78, 99
Nichols, Charles A., 7, 15–16
Night Must Fall, 117
"Noah's Dove," 151
"No One Here But Me" (song by Jones),
  64, 68
Nugie, John, 69

O

O'Brien, Darcy, 102
O'Brien, George, 93–94, 102
Ogston, Helen, 63–64, 69
Ogston, Ted, 50–52
Olander, Phil, 160
Old West era, 141, 153–154, 156
"Ol' Kit Carson" (song by Jones), 141
Oriental Theater, 88
Outlaw Territory, 111

P

Pacific Coast Borax Company, 42, 67
Parade, 90
Parker, Fess, 116
"Peace Within" (song by Jones), 156
Peck, Gregory, 61–62, 116, 117
Perryman, Lloyd, 88, 99, 109, 137, 158
Petaluma, California, 17, 20
Petaluma Argus Courier, 147
Phelps Dodge Corporation, 2, 3, 4, 5
Pipkin, Ann, 45, 55, 91
Pipkin, George, 45, 50–52, 86, 99
Poehlmann, Harold, 20, 143
Poehlmann, Keith, 22, 107
Poehlmann, Max, 17, 21
President's Committee on Employment of
  the Physically Handicapped, 151

Preston, John, 36
Putnam, George, 158–159
Putnam, George Palmer, 52, 59–60, 67–68

R

radio industry, 8, 99. *See also specific programs*
Ramrods, The, 170
"Rangers' Hymn" (song by Jones), 138
Ravenscroft, Thurl, 136, 142
RCA Victor Records, 74, 86, 87
Real McCoys, The, 153–154
Record Producer's Corporation, 153
"Red Rose In The Garden, A," (song by Jones), 64, 68
Reed, Allen, 117, 129, 131–132, 145–146, 161
Reed, Brent, 145, 146
Reed, Shirley, 117, 131, 141, 145–146
Regimental Singers, The, 101
religious themes in Jones's songs, 137, 138–139, 142, 172
"Resurrectus" (poem by Jones), 159
Riders in the Sky (band), 164
Riders in the Sky (film), 89, 157
"Riders in the Sky (A Cowboy Legend)." *See* "Ghost Riders in the Sky" (song by Jones)
"Riders in the Sky Picture To Be Made At John Slaughter Ranch" *(Douglas Daily Dispatch),* 156
Ringo, Johnny, 100
Rio Grande, 97, 101–102, 111, 141
RKO Studios, 59, 94
Rogers, George, 12, 16, 159
Rogers, John, 12, 143
Rogers Ranch, Arizona, 12, 14, 97
"Roll Along" (song by Jones), 146
"Rollin' Dust" (song by Jones), 94, 141
Roostaires, 147
Rough, Tough West, The, 106
"Rough Wrangler" (song by Jones), 112
Russian tour by Jones, 148
Ryan, Matt, 43
Rynning, Thomas, 11

S

"Sacajawea" (song by Jones), 141
"Saddle Up" (song by Jones), 142
San Francisco Chronicle, 68

San Francisco Gay Men's Chorus, 163
Schenk, Aubrey, 106
Scott, Randolph, 60–61
"Searchers, The," (song by Jones), 112–113, 171
Searchers, The, (film by Ford), 102, 112, 155
Sedona, appreciation of, 131, 132, 146
"Sedona, Arizona" (song by Jones), 126–127
Settlers Day Rodeo Parade, 120–121
"Shadows of My Heart, The," (song by Jones), 111
Sheriff of Cochise, 118–119
sign-making as ranger, 35–36, 38, 39, 69
Simonson, Ernest W., 7, 16
Sinatra, Frank, 81
Singing Ranger. *See* Jones, Stanley Davis
"Sky Rider, The," (airplane), 87
Slaughter, "Texas" John, 98
Slaughter Ranch (Douglas, Arizona), 98
"Snowbells and Echoes" (song by Jones), 64, 68
"So Much To Me" (song by Jones), 106
"Song of the Trail" (song by Jones), 138
"Songs of the Dance Hall Girls" (song by Jones), 141
Songs of the National Parks (album by Jones), 133, 135–142
songwriting, 24, 38–39, 88, 94–95, 125–126, 169. *See also specific titles*
Sons of Old Aunt Dinah, The, 116
"Sons of the Mountains" (song by Jones), 138
Sons of the Pioneers, 64, 75, 87, 99, 101–102, 112, 142, 168
Spiderbait, 163–164
Standard School Broadcast, The, 149
"Stan Jones, But 17 Years of Age, Writes Manuscript Accepted by Youth's Companion" *(Douglas Daily Dispatch),* 18–19
Stan Jones and His Death Valley Rangers, 84
Stan Jones and the Ranger Chorus, 136, 137
Stan Jones Day, 120, 129, 147
Stan Jones Fan Club, 129–130
Steel Trap, The, 106
storytelling
      about "Ghost Riders in the Sky" inspiration, 13–15, 98, 165–166, 169
      acquiring the art of, 6, 11–12
      biographical fabrications by Jones, 97, 99–101, 127–128

Stovepipe Wells Hotel, 46–47, 52, 56, 59
St. Stephen's Episcopal Church (Douglas, Arizona), 7, 16, 97, 158, 159
Stuart, Keeter (great nephew), 119–120, 145, 171–172
Sturges, John, 59, 60, 111
"Sweet Bread" (song by Jones), 106

T

Tarzana, California, 116, 132, 144–145, 148–149
television industry, 105, 111. *See also specific shows*
Ten Who Dared, 146–147
Texas John Slaughter, 98–99, 141
30,000 On The Hoof (Grey), 106
This Is Your FBI, 87
This Was The West (album by Jones), 141–142, 151
3 Godfathers, 56–57, 58–59
Tice, Carl, 36, 37–38
Time (magazine), 76, 77, 167
Tiomkin, Dimitri, 106, 112
Traveling Wilburys, 163
Tribute to a Bad Man, 112
Trona Argonaut, 99
Truman, Harry S., 36–37
Twentieth Century Fox, 55, 61
"Two Front Teeth," 74, 75
Two Miles East of Heaven (film by Jones), 117

U

Universal Studios, 106
U.S. Department of the Interior, 37, 106
U.S. Marshal, 120, 122
U.S. Navy, 20–24, 27–28
USS *San Francisco*, 22, 24

V

van Moort, J. G. J., 159
Vargas, Pedro, 75
Villa, Pancho, 1, 100, 127

W

Wagon Master, 94–96, 101, 141
"Wagons West" (song by Jones), 141
Walker, Turnley, 159
Walking Hills, The, 59–61
Walsh, Helen. *See* Jones, Helen Walsh
Walt Disney Company, 98, 116, 132–133, 135, 141, 149–151
Walt Disney Presents, 98
Warner, William, 17, 20, 21
Watts, Levi "Capp," 12–15, 16, 98, 155, 157, 165, 167
"Wayfaring Stranger, The" (song and radio show by Ives), 71
Wayne, John, 56–59, 101
We Believe (play by Jones), 149
Western, Johnny, 88, 109, 158, 160–161, 168
Westlake, Montgomery, 20
Westward Ho The Wagons!, 116
We The People, 65–66
"When Johnny Comes Marching Home," 167–168, 169
Whirlwind (film by Autry), 105
"Whirlwind" (song by Jones), 88, 89, 105
White, Josh, 60, 71
"Wild Hunt, The," legend, 165–166, 167
Wildrose summer headquarters (Death Valley National Monument), 42–45, 67
William Morris Agency, 83, 89, 105
Wirth, Conrad, 137
Wonderful World of Disney, 141
"Woodsman's Prayers" (song by Jones), 138
World War II, 28, 33, 37
Wright, Tommy, 6
"Wringle Wrangle" (song by Jones), 116, 126

Y

Yeager, W. Ward, 34, 35, 36, 37–38
Yellow Sky (film by Wellman), 61–62
"Yellow Stripes" (song by Jones), 111, 141
"You And Me and The Ol' Houn' Dog" (song by Jones), 64, 68
Your Hit Parade, 79
Youth's Companion, The, 18–19, 24

ABOUT THE AUTHOR

© Jay Dusard

After living and working in Death Valley for both the Fred Harvey Company and the National Park Service from 1977 through 1991, Michael K. Ward decided it was time for a move to Tucson to cool off a bit. He has worked as a field technician at Saguaro National Park since 1992. He can be reached at mkward.grits@gmail.com.